Xi Zhu, Thomas R. H. MacClatchie

Confucian Cosmogony

a translation of section forty-nine of the complete Works of the philosopher

Choo-Foo-Tze

Xi Zhu, Thomas R. H. MacClatchie

Confucian Cosmogony
a translation of section forty-nine of the complete Works of the philosopher Choo-Foo-Tze

ISBN/EAN: 9783337256203

Printed in Europe, USA, Canada, Australia, Japan

Cover: Foto ©Thomas Meinert / pixelio.de

More available books at **www.hansebooks.com**

CONFUCIAN COSMOGONY.

A TRANSLATION

OF

SECTION FORTY-NINE OF THE "COMPLETE WORKS"

OF THE

Philosopher Choo-Foo-Tze,

WITH

EXPLANATORY NOTES.

BY THE

Rev. THOS. M'CLATCHIE, M.A.,

CANON OF ST. JOHN'S CATHEDRAL, HONGKONG; AND MISSIONARY FROM THE C.M.S. TO CHINA.

SHANGHAI:
AMERICAN PRESBYTERIAN MISSION PRESS.
LONDON: TRÜBNER AND Co., 60 PATERNOSTER ROW.

MDCCCLXXIV.

PRINTED AT THE PRESBYTERIAN MISSION PRESS AND TYPE FOUNDRY.

LIFE OF CHOO-FOO-TSZE.

The writings of Choo-tsze come next to the Classics in the opinion of the Chinese. "As regards the learning of Confucius, Choo alone," say the Chinese historians, "fully comprehended its true import; and has transmitted it to future generations so perfect and immaculate, that were Confucius himself, or any of the ancient Sages to come back to life, they would not alter what he has written."[1] "In discussing the meaning of 鬼神 Kwei Shin," says Dr. Medhurst, "we shall be greatly aided by the analyzation of a treatise on the subject by 朱夫子 Choo-foo-tsze, the learned commentator on the Four Books, and the elucidator of the five Classics, who, by fixing the sense of the standard writings of the Chinese, has created, as it were the mind of China, and established a system from which all subsequent writers have borrowed, and according to which all modern essayists must be conformed, or they cannot succeed at the literary examinations, through which alone distinction and power can be attained. The opinions of Choo-foo-tsze, therefore, constitute the orthodoxy of China, and all who differ from him are considered heterodox, insomuch that some modern writers, who have dared to dissent from his views, have not only failed in obtaining office, but have also been prevented, through fear of persecution, from publishing their lucubrations."[2]

This philosopher flourished during the Sung Dynasty. He was born A. D. 1130, in the reign of Kaou-tsung at Hwuy-chow, in the province of Ngan-hwuy; and died A. D. 1201 at the age of 71. His father was a Member of the Board of Office. It is related that when Choo-tsze was only four years of age, his father, pointing to the sky, pronounced the word "Heaven," whereupon the child, to the father's astonishment, asked the question, "What is there above it?" At eight years of age he mastered

---
1. Chin. Rep. Vol. xviii, p. 204. 2. Theol. of the Chinese, p. 102.

the Hëaou King which treats of filial duties, and wrote upon the cover of the volume, "If I cannot conform to these lessons, I shall never be a man." His favourite occupations, when other children were at play, were, it is said, either drawing diagrams or sitting in silent contemplation. When ten years old, having read the statement of Mencius, that "Sages are of the same race with me," he rejoiced that it was easy to become a sage. At the age of fourteen his father died, leaving him to the guardianship of Lëw Mëen-che, whose daughter he afterwards married.

When Choo-tsze was eighteen years of age, he took the first literary degree of Sëw-tsae, and in the following year he took the degree of Ken-jin. Shortly afterwards he visited his native village in Woo-yuen, and sacrificed at the tombs of his ancestors. When twenty-two he received his first official appointment as Assistant Magistrate at Tung-an near Amoy; and it was at this time that he devoted himself to the study of Philosophy. He studied the Classics diligently, and also the systems of the Buddhists and Taouists; but on the expostulation of his master, who advised him to confine himself exclusively to the works of the ancient sages, he gave up the two latter branches of study and applied himself to the Classics alone and to searching after true principles. He diligently performed his official duties, superintended the schools in his district, repaired those school houses and colleges which had fallen into decay, and built a library for the benefit of the students. He also revised the rules which related to the sacrifices offered to Confucius. When he retired from the magistracy, the scholars and other inhabitants of the district of Tung-an, subscribed together and erected a sacrificial court for him in the public college. In the year 1164 Choo-tsze was summoned to court by the Emperor, who granted him an audience in the Shwuy-kung palace. On this occasion he presented three memorials; the first inculcated the diligent study of the Classics, and denounced the systems of the Buddhists and Taouists; the second censured the prime minister for making peace with the Mongolians; and the third objected to the interference of the eunuchs Tsang and Lung in state affairs. The Emperor, it is said, was so displeased with the second and third memorials that he refused to continue the audience.

In the year 1179 Choo-tsze was appointed Governor of Nan-kang in the province of Keang-se, where he built a sacrificial court in honour of the philosopher Ling-ke, and rebuilt the college in the valley of the White Deer. He also purchased lands for the support of the scholars; established a code of collegiate rules; and frequently visited the college for the purpose of instructing the students, in consequence of which many of them rose to eminence. In 1181, he petitioned the Emperor with regard to certain corrupt practices amongst high officials, and His Majesty on reading the memorial, which was drawn up in obedience to the Imperial command is said to have become greatly incensed, and to have exclaimed, "So he regards me as lost!" In 1182 he was appointed Superintendant of the revenue derived from the taxation of tea and salt, in the eastern part of Chĕ-keang, and shortly afterwards he was sent to take charge of the government of the department of Shaou-hing in the same province. During the following year he made a tour of the entire district under his jurisdiction, and travelled over dreary mountains and through sequestered valleys, carrying his luggage himself, and visiting all the subordinates under his charge without previous notice. Those whom he found unfaithful he reported to the Emperor with a view to their dismissal. His Majesty was so much pleased that he is reported to have observed to his Prime Minister, that "the government of Choo is truly worthy of admiration." A sacrificial court which had been erected to the honour of an infamous Minister, in Yung-kea, was demolished by his orders. During one of his tours of inspection, he received complaints against a magistrate who was related to the Prime Minister, and he memorialized the Emperor so strongly that the offender was deprived of his office as Commissioner of Justice, and that appointment was offered to Choo-tsze, who decidedly declined it, declaring that to accept it would be like "carrying off as booty the ox which had chanced to tread upon one's field." Shortly after this, Choo-tsze, being attacked and maligned by a Censor whom the Prime Minister had recommended to office, resolved to retire from public life: and an order having, in the mean time, been sent to him from Court, to return home and repair his ancestral temples, he went into retirement and closed his doors against all intruders.

In the year 1191, the Emperor Kwang-tsung appointed Choo-tsze prefect of Chang-chow. The manners and customs of the people under his jurisdiction there, were much deteriorated. Some neglected to wear mourning on the death of their parents. The women frequented Buddhist monasteries to perform religious rites; and some left their homes in order to become nuns. Choo-tsze strictly prohibited all these practices. He also printed copies of the Five Classics and the Four Books, and circulated them amongst the people. Addressing one of his pupils on a certain occasion, he remarked, "When I commenced the study of philosophy, there were many principles which I never expected to master; but now I find that every doubt regarding them has gone." So great was the progress which Choo-tsze had made in the study of the writings of Confucius. On receiving the appointment of Imperial Essayist and Reader to the Emperor Ning-tsung, one of his disciples remarked that His Majesty administered the government with a pure heart, and asked his Master what he considered as requiring chief attention? Choo-tsze replied, "Such is the state of affairs at present, that nothing short of a great and thorough reform will suffice to move the Mind of Heaven, or to rejoice the hearts of men. As to myself, I know it to be my duty to act with the utmost degree of sincerity and assiduity. For any thing further than this, it is not my province to be concerned."

"Under ordinary circumstances, Choo was accustomed," as his biographer states, "to rise before day, dress in plain clothes, a broad cap, and square-toed shoes, and then to worship at the domestic shrine, and at that of the ancient sages; then, to repair to his study, where his chairs, tables &c. must all be in order and his books and writing utensils in their proper places. At his meals, he ordered that the table furniture, and the dishes of soup and rice should all be arranged in a certain order, and that his chopsticks and spoons should have their fixed places. When fatigued by study he would rest himself, closing his eyes and sitting erect; and when refreshed, he would rise and with measured steps walk about for relaxation. At midnight he would retire, and if he chanced to awake in the night, he would wrap himself up in a quilt and sit in bed, sometimes until daylight. His countenance was grave and manly; his speech loud and distinct, his gait easy and dignified; he sat straight and erect; and his whole manner and bearing were impressive. From youth to age, in summer and in winter, and in all the vicissitudes of time and place, he never for a moment departed from this manner of life'" In the third month of the year 1201 Choo-tsze fell sick; and on the day on which he died, having ordered his attendants to place his bed in the central hall, he rose about noon and sat erect; and then, adjusting his hat and dress he quietly lay down and died.

A list of the philosopher's works is given by his biographer Kaou-yu; see *Chinese Repository*, vol. xviii, p. 206, from which the above sketch of his life is abridged.

INTRODUCTION.

The reasonings of the Pagan Philosophers throughout Heathendom, invariably led to the adoption of *two* eternals, viz., God and Matter. Hence it is that in all Heathen systems, the Primordial Matter is regarded as a second God; because, being considered eternal, it cannot but be esteemed Divine; for, eternity is an attribute of Divinity. These systems thus invariably leading to the adoption of *two* eternal Beings, the difficulty has always been how they were to be disposed of. A very ancient, and probably the oldest theory on the subject, was that which united the two together in one whole, making this union as intimate as that of the Mind and body in Man. However this theory may have been slightly modified by different sects of philosophers, one thing is certain, namely, that as Matter was regarded as eternal and animated, no personal God wholly distinct and separate from Matter, can be found in Pagan writings.

The Chinese philosophers are no exception to this rule; for, they hold the eternity of the Primordial Matter, which, in common with Anaximenes, they consider to be Air (氣), and a God (θεος—神). And as the animating Principle of the whole Universe is stated in the Yih King, the most ancient Confucian Classic, to be inherent in this Air, it is plain that there is no such thing as a personal God wholly separate from Matter, to be found in the Confucian Classics; and any attempt therefore to find in them such a Being as the Jehovah of the Scriptures, can only end in disappointment. The Shang-te (上帝) of the Confucian Classics, who, like the daw in the fable, is decked out by his worshippers in certain attributes which belong solely to the true God, is merely, (like his counterpart Jupiter) the animated subtile ether endowed with "Intellect and Sensation." This "Great Monad" (太一) who, as Confucius himself tells us "*divides* in order to form Heaven and Earth, and *gyrates* in order to produce Light and Darkness," is merely the Monad of Pythagoras, and no amount of attributes, however high-sounding, can ever exalt so material a thing into the throne of the true God.

In consequence of this union of God and Matter, all Pagan Philosophers regard the Kosmos or Universe, made from this source, as animated. The Heaven, the Earth, the Sea, Sun, Moon, Stars, Mountains, Trees, &c., are all animated by the one soul which pervades the entire world; so that, this Kosmos, is "One and yet all things, all things and yet one." As one animated whole it is called "Heaven" in all systems, and is declared to be the highest Numen and a Great Man, while Man is said to be a Microcosm. Man therefore is the Key, not merely to the system of Confucius, but also to all other Pagan systems throughout Heathendom.

According to the Greeks and Romans, for instance, Man was regarded as a compound of mind and matter; matter being the body, and Mind being the Soul, the Ruler of the Body; secondly, the Body was regarded as twofold, viz., the head or superior portion, and the feet including the lower part, the inferior portion; thirdly, the Mind or Soul was also twofold, partly rational and partly irrational or Sentient, the former ruling chiefly in the head, but nevertheless pervading the whole body. Lastly, there was another principle in Man, according to these philosophers, which was superior to, and totally distinct although never separate from Mind, viz. Reason. Without *this*, Mind would cease to be Mind, and without Mind, which was always regarded as a portion of pure ether, Reason would be but an abstract idea, and would have no vehicle through which to act. This Reason was regarded as the first God ($\Theta\epsilon o\varsigma$ or Deus $\kappa\alpha\tau$' $\epsilon\xi o\chi\eta\gamma$), and Mind, in which it was inherent, was called $\theta\epsilon o\varsigma$ or deus in consequence of this inherent Divine Reason or God. This, these philosophers transferred to the animated Kosmos or "Heaven." Of this Being, Heaven was the head, Earth and Hades the feet, the Sun and Moon the eyes, the subtile fiery ether the Mind or Rational Soul, the grosser Air the Irrational portion of the soul; and the Hegemonikon or Ruling place of the Divine Reason which pervaded the whole, was Mind or the subtile ether which was regarded as the second $\theta\epsilon o\varsigma$ or Deus, the Demiurgic Ruler and framer of the Kosmos. This Mind or second God is he whom "the generations of men take for the First, they looking up no higher than to the immediate architect of the world."[1] This idea of an animated Kosmos is *confessedly* taken from Man. Plotinus, for instance, thus states the opinion of the ancient philosophers on this point: "It is absurd to affirm that Heaven (or the World) is inanimate or devoid of life and soul, when we ourselves, who have but a part of the mundane body in us are endued with soul. For, how could a part have life and soul in it, the whole being dead and inanimate?"[2]

The Confucian system as given in the text of the Classics, is precisely similar to this. In the Yih King, the great authority on Cosmogony, and the oldest Chinese book in existence, the Kosmos or "Heaven" is declared to be a Great Man, and its eight portions are stated to correspond to eight parts of the human body; *e. gr*.; *Khëen* (Heaven) is the head; *Khwān* (Earth) is the bowels (and womb); *Ching* is the feet; *Seuen* is the thighs; *Kan* is the ears; *Le* is the eyes; *Kān* is the hands; and *Tuy* is the mouth."[3]

Man, according to the Confucianists, is a compound of Mind and Body, Mind being the Ruler; secondly, the body they regard as twofold, the head being the superior portion, and the feet and lower part the inferior portion; thirdly, the Mind or Soul is also twofold, partly Rational (魂) and partly Irrational or Sentient (魄), the former ruling chiefly in the head and upper portion of the body, yet pervading the whole being. Lastly, inherent in this Mind is the Divine Reason, which "makes Mind to be Mind." Mind is pure ether, while the sentient portion of this soul is grosser Air; and the Divine Reason is designated the First God (至神); the God who adorns all things" of the Yih King) and unites with the Rational Soul, the subtile Ether, which is therefore styled God (神); and this latter, in the Kosmos, is the second God or "Mind" or *Shang-te* "the Supreme Emperor;" the Demiurgic Ruler and framer of all things. All this is transferred from Man to the Kosmos which is designated "Heaven," and is declared to be a "Great Man," while Man is regarded as "a little Hea-

---

1. Cud. i, 484.   2. Ibid. ii, 176.
3. Bk. iv., ch. ix.

ven" or Microcosm. This parallel is exact, and the animated ether or *Shang-te* is precisely the same in every respect as the animated ether or Jupiter. Both these Gods are the Light, the firstborn from chaos; both are designated "Mind," and both are the Rational soul of the Kosmos; *Shang-te* being "the 神 of Heaven," and Jupiter being the θεος (or dens) of Heaven; the three terms 神, θεος, and deus, being thus alike applied to *the soul* of the Kosmos.

The Greeks designated their First God (Θεος) Fate, Reason, Nature &c., and regarded Him as an Indivisible Unity; and the Confucianists designate their First God (神) Fate, Reason, Nature, &c., and regard Him as an Indivisible Unity. Plato designates this God "the Adorner," and the Yih King designates Him "He who adorns (妙) the myriad of things."[1] Mind or the second God, the Greeks designated Demon-god (Δαίμων-θεος), and this same Mind the Confucianists also designate Demon-god (鬼 神) Amongst the Greeks and Romans the Rational soul was derived from this ethereal Mind and was therefore designated θεος, deus, or God: and in the Confucian Classics the Rational soul is said to be derived from the same ethereal Mind, and is therefore designated 神 or God. In a word, every part of the Kosmos and every thing which the Greeks and Romans respectively designated "Demon," that the Confucianists also designate "Demon;" and every thing which the former designated θεος or Deus, that the latter designate 神. Any argument, therefore, supposed to prove that the term 神 means "spirit" and not "God," must also be admitted to prove that the terms θεος and Deus mean "Spirit" and not "God." These three terms must necessarily bear precisely the same meaning for the reasons stated. The fact that the Chinese term 神, (like θεος or Deus) is the designation of that which pervades and animates the το παν must be regarded as proof that this term means "God" in the sense of that term as used by all pagan philosophers, and not pure "Spirit," of which latter, in fact, *they know nothing whatever*.

Plate I will assist the student to understand what has been stated as to the animated Kosmos.

---

1. Bk. iv, ch. vi.

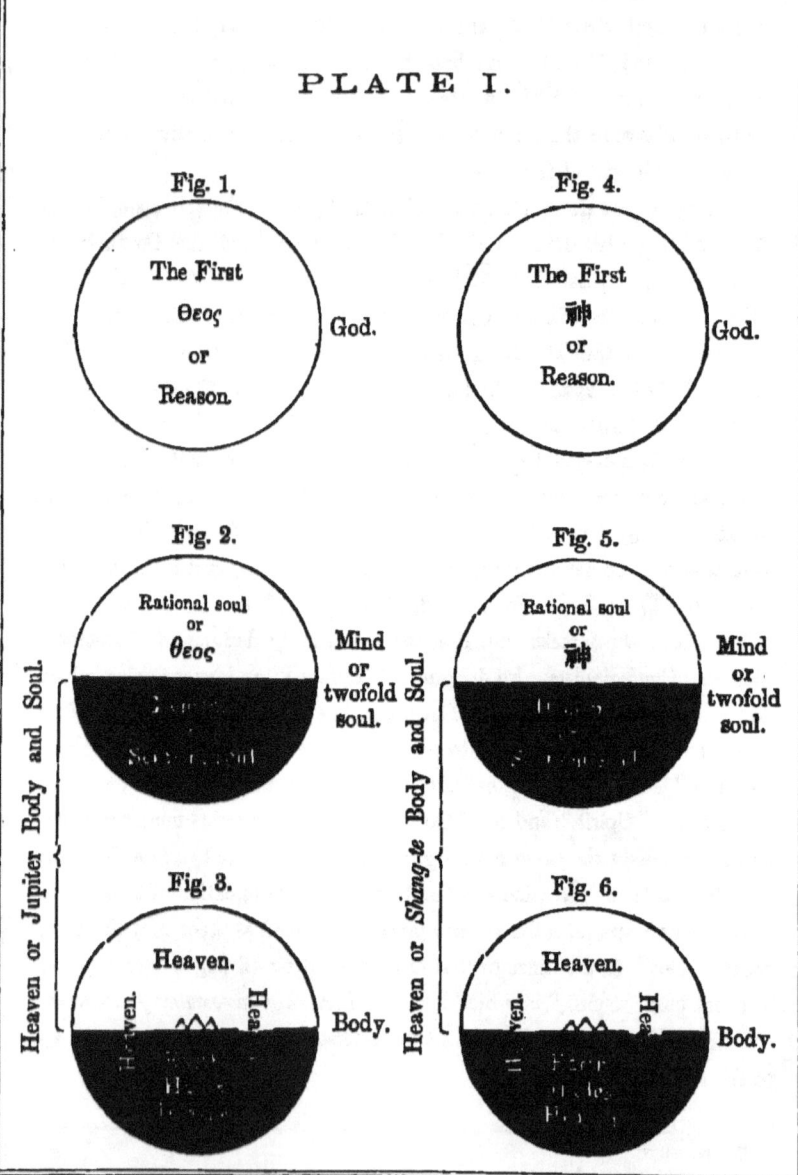

EXPLANATION OF PLATE I.

Figs. 1, 2, and 3, placed one over the other (*i.e.* 3 over 2, and both over 1) so as to form one globe, give the Greek Kosmos or Man complete; and Figs. 4, 5, and 6, placed in the same way give the Confucian Kosmos or Man complete.

Fig. 3, placed over fig. 2, gives the Mind (fig. 2), and Body (fig. 3), of the Kosmos or Man according to the Greeks (and Romans by substituting *Deus* for $\theta\varepsilon o\varsigma$); and fig. 6 placed over fig. 5, gives the Mind and Body of the Kosmos or Man according to the Confucianists.

In both systems Mind (figs. 2, and 5), is twofold, partly Rational and partly sentient.

Figs. 3. and 6, represent the visible world which is all "Heaven" in both systems. The Earth is represented by a mountain, because the highest mountain, the abode of the Gods, is, in both systems, supposed to be the first land which appears as each chaotic deluge subsides.

In both cases the animated Kosmos (fig. 2 inherent in fig. 3, and fig. 5 inherent in fig. 6) is merely the First Man in his Mundane or deified character. He is deified by making his soul the Deity Himself, or the Divine Reason (figs. 1 and 4 inherent in figs. 2 and 5 respectively); the Hegemonikon being the Rational portion of the soul.

"In endeavouring to define the terms employed by Chinese authors, we must also bear in mind their theory that 人爲小天地 man is a microcosm, or heaven and earth in miniature."*

---

* Theol of Chinese, p. 2.

PLATE II.

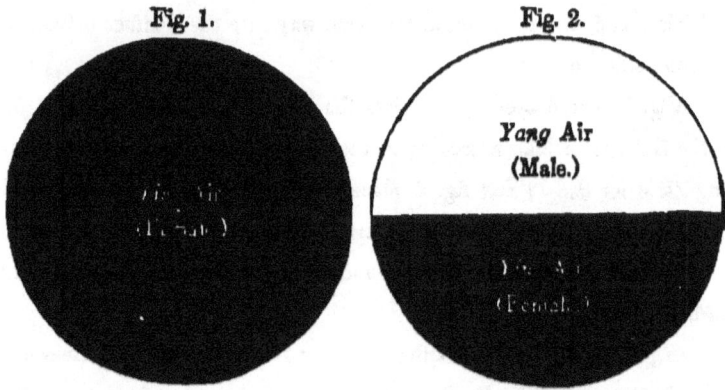

Fig. 1.   Fig. 2.

Fig. 1 represents the whole infinite mass of Primordial Air when in Chaos. This is the Great Monad (太一) or *Shang-te* before he divides into two Airs, a Male and a Female, to generate the World. He is also called the Great Beginning (太初); and is both the Fœtus of Man, and the *Ovum Mundi*. Inherent in this "Mind" is the Divine Reason. See Plate I., Fig. 4.

Fig. 2 represents this mass of Primordial Air divided into Subtile and Gross; or Light and Darkness.

INTRODUCTION. XV

PLATE III.

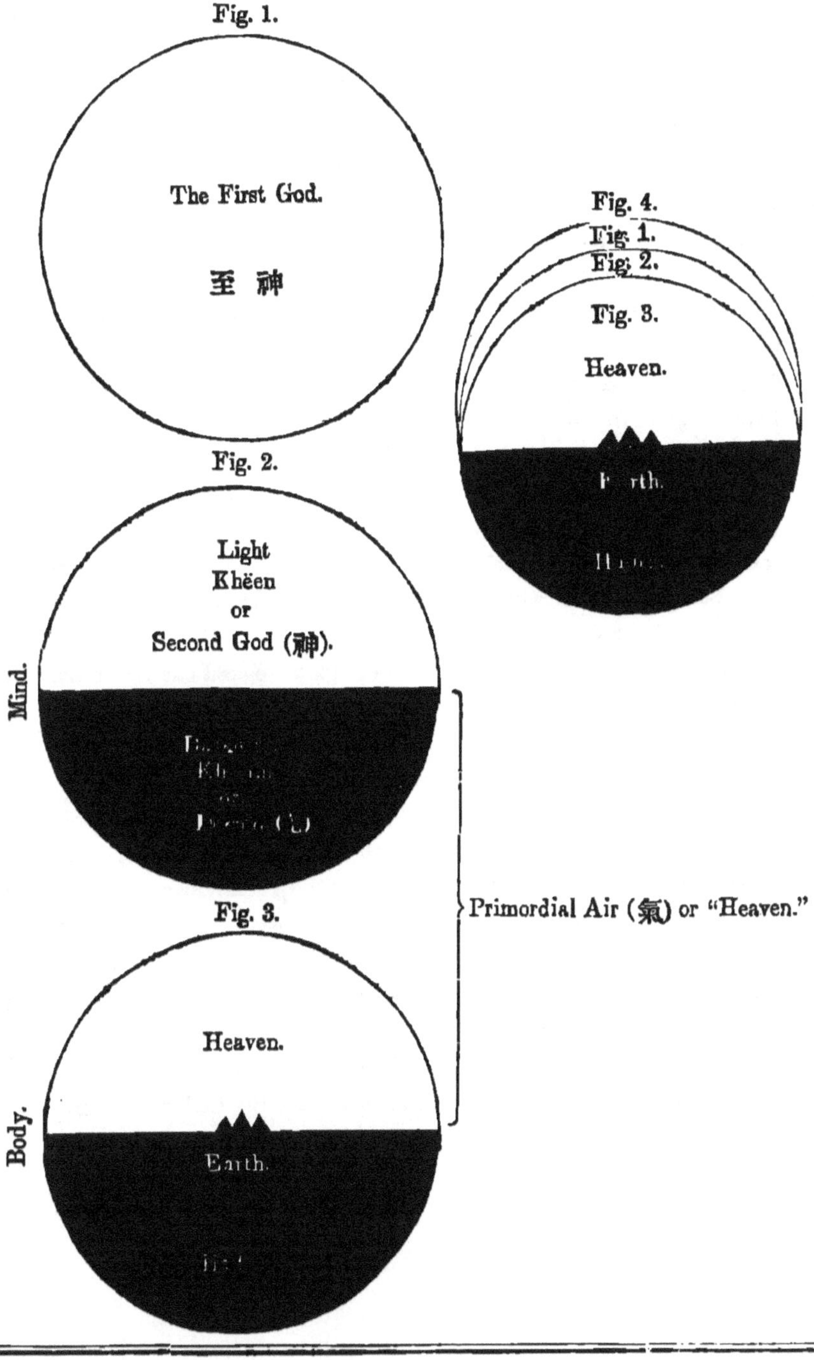

Fig. 1.

The First God.

至神

Fig. 2.

Light
Khëen
or
Second God (神).

Image
Khëen
or
Second (?)

Mind.

Fig. 3.

Heaven.

Earth.

Body.

Fig. 4.
Fig. 1.
Fig. 2.
Fig. 3.

Heaven.

Earth.

} Primordial Air (氣) or "Heaven."

EXPLANATION OF PLATE III.

The Complete Shang-te, (上 帝).

Fig. 1 represents the First God who is styled Fate, Incorporeal Reason, The Infinite, The Good, The (Incorporeal) Great Extreme, Nature the Adorner, &c. He is the Great Vacum, an Immoveable Mover, Incomprehensible, Omnipresent, an Indivisible Unity, &c.

Figs. 2 and 3 represent the whole mass of the Primordial Air, the subtile and the gross in the arranged Kosmos, in which the first God is inherent, the light being His Hegemonikon. These two circles form the animated Kosmos. Fig 2 is the Mind or twofold soul, partly Rational, and partly sentient (Light and Darkness), the Great Demon-god *Shang-te,* who is said to be "material" compared with fig. 1, but "Spiritual" compared with fig. 3, which is the grosser Air or visible world, the Body of fig. 2. *Shang-te* or the animated Kosmos therefore is composed of figs. 2 and 3, united in one as Body and Soul, and this complete Being or Numen is called "Heaven." "The Great Monad," "The (corporeal) Great Extreme," and (the corporeal portion of) "Nature."

Fig. 4. represents these three circles or globes placed one within the other in order to complete the Being *Shang-te* or the animated Kosmos. The entire description of this Great Numen is as follows: "His bodily form is designated Heaven (fig. 3.), the Ruling power is designated 帝 (fig. 2), the Adorning *Yung* is designated God (神 fig. 1), the essence is designated *Khëen* (Hard)." "Divided and treated of, then, his bodily form is designated Heaven, the Ruling power is designated 帝, the *Kung Yung* is designated Demon-god (fig. 2), the Adorning *Yung* is designated God (神), and the essence is designated *Khëen.* Khëen (Rational soul fig. 2), is the Beginning of the Myriad of things, and hence he is called Heaven, and Light, and Father, and Prince." *Yih King, Bk.* iii, *ch.* xi, *com.* (Kang-he). "Khëen-khwăn (Fig. 2) is the 帝 (*Shang-te*) who governs the Myriad of things and pervades the midst of the Six Children" (three sons, and three daughters,—their three wives: *Yih King Bk.* iv, *ch.* x, *text*). *Ibid. Bk.* iv, *ch.* vi, *com.*

INTRODUCTION.   xvii

The Chinese arrangement of the diagrams is as follows:—

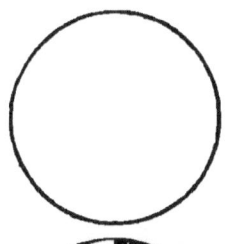

This Circle is 無極 or "The Infinite" (απειρον); the "First God."

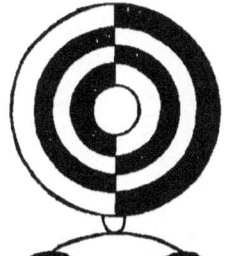

陽動   陰靜

This second circle is 太極 The Great Extreme or the whole mass of Primordial Air 氣. The small circle in the centre represents the first circle which is inherent in this one and is the 中庸 of Confucius.

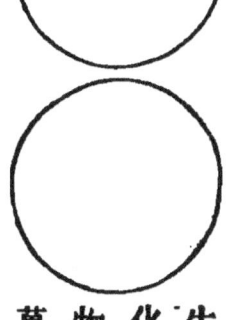

The Five Elements generated from the preceding.

乾道成男   坤道成女

A male and a female generated from second circle; and contained in the one circle of the Kosmos, which is therefore a great Hermaphrodite.

萬物化生

The Myriad of things generated from second circle.

All these constitute but one circle or Kosmos, which is "One yet All Things."

SEC. XLIX OF THE COMPLETE WORKS OF CHOO-TSZE.

淵鑒齋

御纂朱子全書卷四十九

理氣

　　總論

天下未有無理之氣亦未有無氣之理。

有是理後生是氣自一陰一陽之謂道推來此性自有仁義。

先有箇天理了却有氣氣積爲質而性具焉。

問先有理抑先有氣曰理未嘗離乎氣然理形而上者氣形而下者自形而上下言豈無先後理無形氣便粗有渣滓。

THE COMPLETE WORKS OF CHOO-TSZE.

IMPERIAL EDITION.

SECTION XLIX.

PART I.

FATE AND AIR.—THE GENERAL TREATISE.

Paragraph, 1. In the whole Universe there is no such thing as Air without Fate, or Fate without Air.

2. This Fate existing, then this Air is generated. This follows from (the statement in the Yih King that), "The alternating *Yin* and *Yang* is Reason."* This Nature (that is Fate inherent in Air), is spontaneously Benevolent and Upright.

3. This Heavenly Fate first existing, then most certainly the Air exists. The Air when accumulated forms Substance, and Nature is then complete.

4. Being asked whether Fate or Air is prior in point of time, he replied, Fate is never separate from the Air, but Fate is Incorporeal, while the Air is Corporeal. In this respect, therefore, is there not priority and posteriority? Fate is Incorporeal, while the Air is coarse and has dregs.

---

* Choo-tsze's commentary on this passage is: "The revolving *Yin* and *Yang* is the Air; the inherent Fate is that which is designated Reason." The *Yin* and *Yang* are merely the two divisions of the Primordial Air. The Air establishes the inherent Reason by acting as a Receptacle for it; and the inherent Reason (or Fate or Nature), gives name to the whole compound. Hence the Primordial Air is merely the ethereal vehicle of the inherent Fate or Reason—the *Melior Natura*.

理氣本無先後之可言。然必欲推其所從來則須說先有是理。然又非別為一物。即存乎是氣之中。無是氣則是理亦無掛搭處氣則為金木水火理則為仁義禮智

問理與氣曰伊川說得好曰理一分殊合天地萬物而言只是一個理及在人則又各自有一個理

有是理便有是氣但理是本而今且從理上說。如云太極動而生陽。動極而靜靜而生陰。不成動已前便無靜程子曰動靜無端蓋此亦是且自那動處說起。若論著動以前又有靜。靜以前又有動

如云一陰一陽之謂道。繼之者善也。這繼字便是動之端。若只一開一闔而無繼。便是闔殺了。又問繼是動靜之間否。曰是靜之終

5. Strictly speaking, we cannot predicate priority or posteriority, as regards time, of Fate or the Air. Yet, if we treat concerning origin, then we must say that Fate has the priority. Nevertheless Fate is not a separate thing, it is preserved in the midst of the Air; if the Air did not exist, then this Fate would not have any thing to rest upon. The Air is Metal, Wood, Water, and Fire; Fate is Benevolence, Rectitude, Propriety and Wisdom.

6. Being asked about Fate and the Air conjointly, he said: E-chuen expresses the matter well when he says, that Fate is Unity but its parts are diverse. Heaven, Earth, and the myriad of things collectively are just one whole Fate. With regard to Man, each has his own Fate within him.

7. Fate existing, then the Air exists, yet Fate is the Root. Now, speaking from Fate as a commencement, as for instance when it is said "The Great Extreme moved and generated the Light; having moved to the utmost it rested, and resting, generated the Darkness;" then, previous to Motion was there no rest? Ching-tsze says, Motion and Rest have no commencement; this also is speaking from the place of Motion as a commencement. If it be said that before Motion there was Rest, and before that Rest there was Motion, as for instance when it is said (in the Yih King that) "The alternating Light and Darkness is Reason; their pivot of Motion (*i. e.* Reason) is Goodness;" this term "pivot" refers to the commencement of Motion. If there was only one shutting and opening (of the universe), and no "pivot" of perpetual revolutions, then the universe when shut up would perish. Being asked whether this "pivot" is in the centre between Motion and Rest, he replied, that it is the termination of Rest, and the commencement of Motion.

動之始也。且如四時。到得冬月。萬物都歸窠了若不生來年便都息了。蓋是貞復生元無窮如此。

問有是理而後有是氣未有人時此理何在曰也只在這裏如一海水或取得一杓或取得一擔或取得一椀都是這海水但是他爲主我爲客他較長久我得之不久耳。

問理在氣中發見處如何曰如陰陽五行錯綜不失條緒。便是理。

問若氣不結聚時理亦無所附著。

問先有理後有氣之說曰不消如此說而今知得他合下是先有理後有氣耶後有理先有氣耶皆不可得而推究然以意度之則疑此氣是依傍這理行及此氣之聚則理亦在焉蓋氣則能凝結造

Take for instance the Four Seasons. In the Winter the myriad of things return to their resting place, and if there was no further generation, then the following year could not exist. But, because *Ching* again generates *Yuen,* there is no termination to the present state of things.

8. Being asked in reference to the statement, "Fate existing then the Air exists," where this Fate was before Man appeared? He replied, that it was even then in existence, resembling the whole body of water in a sea, from which if we take up a ladle full, or two buckets full, or a bowl full, still it is all the same sea water. However, this Fate is Host while I am but his guest, he, compared with me is eternal, while I obtain him and am mortal.

9. Being asked how this Fate manifests his presence in the midst of the Air, he replied, that it is just this Fate which prevents the Light and the Darkness, and the five Elements from becoming so tangled together as to lose their distinctness (in chaos). If the Air did not accumulate together, then Fate would not have anything to rest upon.

10. Being asked with regard to Fate existing first and the Air existing afterwards, he replied that it is not necessary to state the matter thus. To understand now whether in the One Whole (τὸ πᾶν) Fate exists first and Air afterwards, or the Air first and Fate afterwards, is what we cannot search out. However if I may offer a conjecture, I suppose that the Air depends upon Fate for action and that wherever the Air accumulates, Fate is also there. Now, the Air has the power of condensing and forming things; but Fate neither devises nor plans, nor makes any thing: only, wherever the Air condenses and accumulates, Fate is in the midst of it. And, since

作。理却無情意。無計度。無造作。只此氣凝聚處理便在其中且如
天地間人物草木禽獸其生也莫不有種定不會無種了白地生
出一個物事這個都是氣若理則只是個潔淨空闊底世界無形
迹他却不會造作氣則能醞釀凝聚生物也。
問有是理便有是氣似不可分先後曰要之也先有理只不可說是
今日有是理明日却有是氣也須有先後。
問未有天地之先畢竟是先有理。如何曰未有天地之先畢竟也只
是理。有此理便有此天地若無此理便亦無天地無人無物都無
該載了有理便有氣流行發育萬物曰發育是理發育之否曰有
此理便有此氣流行發育理無形體曰所謂體者是強名否曰是

Men and things, Grass, Trees, Birds and Beasts, in the midst of Heaven and Earth, are all generated from seed, and there is not any one thing without seed, then, when a single thing is produced apparently without seed, this is wholly owing to the Air. With regard to Fate, this is a pure, empty, wide world, without Corporeal traces, it cannot make any thing. The Air possesses the power of fermenting, condensing, and generating things.

11. Being asked whether Fate and Air are so obtained (in the formation of things) that priority and posteriority cannot be predicated of them? He replied, in reality Fate is prior; yet we cannot assert that Fate exists to-day, and Air to-morrow; and yet there must certainly be priority and posteriority.

12. Being asked whether Fate positively existed before Heaven and Earth? He replied, that before the existence of Heaven and Earth there most certainly was just this Fate. Fate existing, then Heaven and Earth existed. If Fate had no existence, then also there could not be any Heaven, or Earth, or Man, or Things; none of these would have any containing receptacle. Fate existing, then the Air exists, flows forth, pervades, generates, and nourishes the myriad of things. Being asked whether it is Fate which produces and nourishes (all things) he replied, that when Fate exists, then the Air exists, flows forth, and pervades, produces, and nourishes; Fate has no bodily form. Being asked whether the word "bodily" is not too strong an expresion to use here, he replied in the affirmative. Another person enquiring whether Fate is Infinite and the Air finite? He replied, with regard to limits, what limit can be assigned to either of them?

13. Some one asking whether Fate exists first in time and the Air afterwards, he replied, that we cannot really

曰理無極氣有極否曰論其極將那處做極。

或問理在先氣在後曰理與氣本無先後之可言但推上去時却如理在先氣在後相似。

可機問大鈞播物還是一去便休也還有去而復來之理曰一去便休耳豈有散而復聚之氣。

問氣之伸屈曰譬如將水放鍋裏煮水既乾那泉水依前又來不得將已乾之水去做他。

問上帝降衷於民天將降大任於人天祐民作之君天生物因其才而篤作善降百祥作不善降百殃天將降非常之禍於此世必預出非常之人以擬之凡此等類是蒼蒼在上者眞有主宰如是耶。

predicate priority or posteriority, as to time, of Fate and the Air; yet if we push the matter up to the highest point of time, then Fate is, as it were, first, and the Air is, as it were, posterior to it.

14. Ko-ke asked whether when the Great Framer has arranged all things, and any thing once departs (out of existence), does it altogether cease to be, or does it merely depart and return again? He replied, once gone it ceases to exist; for, how could Air once scattered, again collect together?

15. Being asked as to the expanding and contracting of the Air, he replied; suppose we take water and boil it in a caldron; then when this water has evaporated, in order that water should return as before, you would not take the already evaporated water to refill the caldron?

16. Being asked about the following statements in the Classics: "*Shang-te* sends down the virtuous Nature upon the people;" "Heaven bestows high official positions upon the deserving;" "Heaven protects the people and appoints princes;" "Heaven generates things, and increases their powers according to their capacity; upon the good it sends down innumerable felicities, and on the evil innumerable calamities;" "When Heaven is about to send down some extraordinary calamity upon the world it first sends forth an extraordinary Man to conjecture it;" whether, in all such statements as these, it is meant that there is really a ruling power in the azure Heaven above, who acts thus; or, that Heaven being without Mind, it is just owing to Fate that matters are so? He replied that

抑天無心只是推原其理如此日此三叚只一意這箇也只是理如此氣運從來一盛了又一衰一衰了又一盛只管恁地循環去無有衰而不盛者。

人呼氣時腹却脹吸氣時腹却厭。論來呼而腹厭吸而腹脹乃是今若此者盖呼氣時此一口氣雖出第二口氣復生故其腹脹及吸氣時其所生之氣又從裏趕出故其腹却厭老子曰天地之間其猶橐籥乎動而不屈虛而愈出橐籥只是今之鞴扇耳。

理搭於氣而行。

以氣言則春夏秋冬以德言則元亨利貞在人則爲仁義禮智元亨利貞。理也有只四叚氣也有只四叚理便在氣中。兩個不曾相離。

問理與數曰有是理便有是氣有是氣便有是數盖數乃是分界限處。

such statements have but one interpretation; it is merely that Fate is so. The revolving Air, from the beginning, has experienced fulness after decline and decline after fulness, ever thus revolving in a circle. There has never been decline without fulness following it.

17. When a man breathes forth, his stomach is distended, and when he draws in his breath it is contracted. With regard to expiration and contraction of the stomach, inspiration and distention of the stomach, the rule is so. Now, since this is the case, then, on expiration, although that portion of breath goes forth, yet, a succeeding portion is again generated, and therefore the stomach is distended. On inspiration, this portion of breath which has been generated is expelled from within, and therefore the stomach contracts. Laou-tsze says, that the midst of Heaven and Earth resembles a Fŭh-yŏ; when in motion, there is no deficiency (of Air); and when empty, more is expelled. The Fŭh-yŏ is the modern bellows.

18. Fate unites with the Air, and pervades.

19. Spring, Summer, Autumn and Winter are the Air; *Yuen, Hăng, Le,* and *Ching* constitute the *virtus* of the Air. In Man this is Benevolence, Rectitude, Propriety and Wisdom. Fate has these four parts *Yuen, Hăng, Le,* and *Ching;* and the Air has four parts. Fate is just in the midst of the Air, and these two can never be separated from each other.

20. Being asked as to the relation between Fate and Number, he replied, that this Fate existing, then the Air exists; and when the Air exists then Number exists; for, enumeration is the assigning of limits.

此身只是個軀殼內外無非天地陰陽之氣如魚在水外面水便是
肚裏水鱖魚肚裏水與鯉魚肚裏水只一般
氣聚成形理與氣合便能知覺如火得脂膏便有許多光燄蓋所覺
者心之理也能覺者氣之靈也
人之所以為人其理則天地之理其氣則天地之氣理無迹不可見
故於氣觀之。以上語類二十三條
天地之間有理有氣理也者形而上之道也生物之本也氣也者
而下之器也生物之具也是以人物之生必禀此理然後有性必
禀此氣然後有形。答黃道夫
所謂理與氣決是二物但在物上看則二物渾淪不可分開各在一
處然不害二物之各為一物也若在理上看則雖未有物而已有

21. My body is just a shell; within and without there is nothing but the Light and Dark Air of Heaven and Earth. This resembles a fish in the water; the water outside is the same as that inside its stomach; and the water inside a whale is the same as the water inside a carp.

22. Accumulated Air produces form; Fate unites with it, and then it possesses the powers of Understanding and Sensation, just as when oil is poured upon fire then there is much flame. That which causes Sensation to exist is the Fate inherent in Mind, and that which possesses the power of Sensation is the spiritual part of the Air (*i. e.* "Mind.")

23. That which makes Man to be Man, is, that his Fate is the Fate inherent in Heaven and Earth, and his Air is the Air of Heaven and Earth. Fate has no traces, and is invisible; and therefore we must look at the Air in order to discern its presence.

24. In the midst of Heaven and Earth, there is nothing but Fate and the Air. Fate is Incorporeal Reason, the Origin of Life; the Air is the Corporeal Vessel, the Receptacle of Life. Hence both Man and Things, at their generation, must receive this Fate and then they have Nature; they must receive this Air, and then they have Form.

25. With regard to Fate and the Air, these are certainly two different things; yet in looking at any thing, the two are blended together, and cannot be so separated as to occupy different places; nevertheless this does not prevent their being totally distinct things. With regard to Fate, then although the Fate of a thing exists before the thing itself has any existence, yet, it is merely the Fate (*i. e.* the idea) which exists and nothing more, the

物之理然亦但有其理而已未嘗實有是物也大凡看此等處須
認得分明又兼始終方是不錯 答劉叔文
有此理後方有此氣旣有此理有安頓處大而天地細而
螻蟻其生皆是如此又何慮天地之生無所付受耶要之理之一
字不可以有無論未有天地之時便已如此了也 答楊志仁
問天地之間有理有氣理常不移而氣不常定中庸曰大德必得其
名必得其位必得其壽理固當如此然孔子無位顏子夭死蓬蓽
之士固有老死而名不著者豈非氣使之然耶故君子道其常而
不道其非常然竊疑理先而氣後今理旣不足以勝氣則凡福善
禍淫之說不驗常多何以爲天地之常經意謂氣雖不同然亦隨
世而異堯舜禹以聖人在上天下平治以和召和則氣亦醇正而

thing itself having as yet no real existence. Every one who considers the matter must clearly discriminate between the two, and must also distinguish between the beginning and the end, and then there can be no mistake.

26. When this Fate is obtained, then this Air is afterwards obtained; and when this Air is obtained, then this Fate has something to rest upon. The generation of great things such as Heaven and Earth, and of small things such as Ants is the same in this respect; for, why should not Heaven and Earth, at their generation have these conferred upon them? As to Fate, we need not discuss its existence or non-existence for it was in existence before Heaven and Earth.

27. Being asked as follows: In the midst of Heaven and Earth there is nothing but Fate and Air. Fate never changes, but the Air is ever changing. The Chung Yung says that "Great merit must obtain reputation, distinguished rank, and long life." Fate certainly ought to be so. Yet, Confucius had no distinguished rank; Yen-tsze died young; and some poor scholars up to the time of their death obtain no renown. Is it not the Air which causes all this? Hence the Model Man discourses about the unchangeable and not about the changeable. Yet, I suppose Fate is prior and the Air posterior to it. At the present time, since Fate cannot conquer the Air, all the statements concerning the happiness of the good and the misery of the wicked are, for the most part unfulfilled. How can this be the constant law of Heaven and Earth? I suppose that although the Air is changeable, yet it changes with the age. In the times of Yaou, Shun and Yu, because Sages were Emperors, the Empire was peaceably governed, and peace induced peace. Then the Air was perfectly pure and followed after Fate. But, as in

隨於理。如春秋戰國之時。刑殺慘酷。則氣亦隨之而變。而理反不能勝此處亦當關於人事否曰此於前叚論性命處已言之矣。雖是所感不同。亦是元氣薄耳。答鄭子上

有是理即有是氣氣則無不兩者故易曰太極生兩儀而老子乃謂道先生一而後一乃生二。則其察理亦不精矣。答程可久

論萬物之一原則理同而氣異觀萬物之異體則氣猶相近而理絕不同也氣之異者粹駁之不齊理之異者偏全之或異幸更詳之。

自當無可疑也。答黃商伯

氣之所聚理即在焉然理終爲主此即所謂妙合也。答王子合

所疑理氣之偏若論本原。即有理然後有氣故理不可以偏全論。若論禀賦則有是氣。而後理隨以具故有是氣則有是理無是理則

the times of Confucius and Mencius there were executions and oppressions, then the Air followed the times and changed so that Fate could not subdue it. Do all these things refer to human affairs? He replied, that he has already treated of this in a previous section on Nature. Although what is received is not the same (in all), yet the Original Air was vitiated in the cases instanced.

28. Fate existing then the Air exists. The Air is always of two sorts, and hence the Yih King states that "The great Extreme generated the two E." Laou-tsze also says that Reason first generated the Monad, and afterwards the Monad generated Two; thus his investigation of Fate is not minute.

29. With regard to the One Origin of all things, then Fate is uniform, but the Air varies. With regard to the varied bodies of the myriad of things, there is a degree of similarity in the Air (of which they are formed), but their Fate is very diverse. The distinction in the Air is that of pure and mixed; and the probable distinction in Fate is partial or complete reception. We have, happily, further investigated this point; we should not remain in doubt about it.

30. Wherever the Air accumulates, Fate is also there inherent in it; but Fate is undoubtedly Lord. This is what is meant by his "adorning the One Whole" *i. e.* the το παν.

31. With regard to any surmise as to the diversity in Fate and the Air; if we speak of the Original, Fountain of being, then, Fate existing the Air existed, and therefore we cannot predicate completeness or incompleteness of Fate with reference to it (*i. e.* the Fountain). But if we treat of the bestowing of this (Fate and Air) upon all things (with a view to their existence), then,

無是理是氣多則是理多。氣少即是理少又豈不可以偏全論耶。答趙致道

理固不可以偏正通塞言然氣禀既殊則氣之偏者便只得理之偏。

氣之塞者便自與理相隔是理之在人亦不能無偏塞也。橫渠論

受光有大小昏明而照納不二其說甚備。答杜仁仲

所論氣禀有偏而理之統體未嘗有異得之明道又謂不可以濁者

不爲水。亦是此意也。答杜仁仲

蓋理則純粹至善卽氣則雜糅不齊。內君子外小人凡所以抑陰而

扶陽者乃順乎理以裁成輔相。而濟夫氣數之不及者也。又何病

乎。答或人

性只是理不可以聚散言所謂精神魂魄有知有覺者皆氣之所爲

having obtained the Air, Fate follows afterwards and is inherent in it. Hence the Air being obtained, then Fate is obtained; where the Air does not exist, there, Fate does not exist; when the Air abounds, then Fate abounds; when the Air is deficient, then Fate is deficient. Can we not thus predicate completeness and incompleteness of them?

32. Intrinsically we cannot predicate perfection or imperfection, freedom or obstruction, of Fate. But, since the Air bestowed on things is diverse, then the Air when imperfect obtains Fate imperfectly; and when the Air is obstructed, then separation from Fate takes places. This Fate when inherent in Man, cannot be free from incompleteness and obstruction. Hwang-k'heu says, that, in the reception of light there is the distinction of much or little, dullness or brilliancy, and yet we do not receive two lights. This illustration is perfect.

33. With regard to what has been said as to the diversity of the Air received, and the sameness of the entire body of Fate the case is so. Ming-taou also says, that which cannot be muddied is not water; this is just the same idea.

34. Fate is perfectly pure and superlatively good; but the Air is mixed and variable. Within is the Model Man, without, the Mean Man. All who keep down the Darkness and bear up the Light, are obedient to Fate, and complete, support, and make up the deficiencies in the Air. What blemish can exist in such a case?

35. Nature is just this Fate, and we cannot predicate accumulation or dispersion of it. In speaking of the Subtile and the Divine (that is to say) the Anima and the Rational Soul having the power of Understanding and Sensation, these are the attributes of the Air; hence when

也。故聚則有散則無若理則初不爲聚散而有無也。但有是理則
有是氣。苟氣聚乎此則其理亦命乎此耳。答廖子晦
理有動靜。故氣有動靜。若理無動靜。則氣何自而有動靜乎。且以
前論之。仁便是動。義便是靜。此又何關於氣乎。答鄭子上 以上文集十三條

it accumulates these powers exist, when it scatters (at death), then they no longer exist. With regard to Fate we cannot speak of its originally accumulating or dispersing, existing or non-existing; only, this Fate existing, then the Air exists; and when the Air accumulates any where, there Fate is also received.

36. Fate possesses Motion and Rest, and therefore the Air possesses Motion and Rest. If Fate had not Motion and Rest, then how could the Air have Motion and Rest? To illustrate this by what is apparent, then Benevolence is Motion, and Rectitude is Rest; what has the Air to do with these?

太極

太極只是一個理字。

問太極不是未有天地之先有個渾成之物是天地萬物之理總名否曰太極只是天地萬物之理在天地言則天地中有太極在萬物言則萬物中各有太極未有天地之先畢竟是先有此理動而生陽亦只是理靜而生陰亦只是理。

萬物四時五行只是從那太極中來太極只是一個氣迤邐分做兩個氣裏面動底是陽靜底是陰又分做五氣又散爲萬物。

問太極解何以先動而後靜先用而後體先感而後寂曰在陰陽言則用在陽而體在陰然動靜無端陰陽無始不可分先後今只就起處言之畢竟動前又是靜用前又是體感前又是寂陽前又是

PART II.

THE GREAT EXTREME.

1. The Great Extreme is just the same as Fate.

2. Being asked whether the Great Extreme is the general name for the Fate inherent in Heaven, Earth, and the myriad of things, and not of the chaotic mass before Heaven and Earth existed; he replied, it is just the Fate inherent in Heaven, Earth, and all things. With regard to its being in Heaven and Earth, then the Great Extreme is in the centre of Heaven and Earth; and with regard to its being in the myriad of things, then the Great Extreme is in the centre of each. Before Heaven and Earth there must first have existed this Fate. That which moved and generated the Light is just this Fate; and that which rested and generated the Darkness is also just this Fate.

3. The myriad of things, the Four Seasons, and the Five Elements just come from the centre of the Great Extreme. The Great Extreme is just one Air which divided obliquely and became two Airs; the part which has motion is the Light, and that which has rest (*vis inertiæ*), is the Darkness. It also divided and became five Airs; scattered, and became all things.

4. Being asked: In your explanation of the Great Extreme, why do you say that first there was motion and afterwards Rest; first activity and then *inertia*; first the exertion of influence, and then the cessation of influence? He replied, with regard to the Light and the Darkness, then activity pertains to the Light, and *inertia* to the Darkness: but, Motion and Rest have no beginning, the

陰而寂前又是感靜前又是動將何者為先後不可只道今日動而昨日靜更不說也如鼻息言呼吸則辭順不可道吸呼便為始而畢竟呼前又是吸吸前又是呼。

太極非是別為一物即陰陽而在陰陽即五行而在五行即萬物而在萬物只是一個理而已因其極至故名曰太極。

若無太極便不翻了天地。

太極理也動靜氣也氣行則理亦行二者常相依而未嘗相離也當初元無一物只有此理有此理便會動而生陽靜而生陰靜極復動動極復靜循環流轉其實理無窮氣亦與之無窮自有天地便是這物事在這裏流轉一日有一日之運一月有一月之運一歲有一歲之運只是這個物事滾將去。

Light and the Darkness have no commencement; we cannot predicate priority or posteriority of them. Now, if we just speak of the place of commencement, then certainly before Motion there is Rest; before activity there is *inertia*, before influence there is non-influence; before Light there is Darkness. Also, before non-influence there is influence; before Rest there is Motion; which then shall we consider prior to the other? We cannot say to-day that Motion is first, and omit all mention of yesterday's Rest. For example, in speaking correctly of breathing, we must say "expiration and inspiration," not "inspiration and expiration," yet assuredly, before expiration there must be inspiration, and before inspiration there must be expiration.

5. The Great Extreme is not a separate thing; it is just the Light and Darkness, and it is in the Light and Darkness; it is the Five Elements, and it is in the Five Elements; it is the myriad of things, and it is in the myriad of things. It is Fate and nothing else: and because it is the extreme point, therefore, it is designated the Great Extreme.

6. If the Great Extreme did not exist, then would not Heaven and Earth turn upside down?

7. The Great Extreme is Fate; that which has Motion and Rest is the Air. When the Air pervades, then Fate also pervades. These two mutually depend upon each other, and cannot be separated from each other. In the beginning, before a single thing existed, there was merely this Fate. When this Fate existed then it moved and generated the Light, rested and generated the Darkness; having rested to the utmost limit, it again moved; and having moved to the utmost limit, it again rested, revolving thus in a perpetual circle. This Fate being really

太極未動之前便是陰。陰靜之中自有陽之根。陽動之中又有陰之根。動之所以必靜者根乎陰故也。靜之所以必動者根乎陽故也。

太極之有動靜是天命之流行也。或疑靜處如何流行。曰惟是一動一靜。所以流行。如秋冬之時謂之不流行可乎。若謂不能流行。何以謂之靜而生陰也。觀生之一字可見。

自太極至萬物化生只是一個道理包括。非是先有此而後有彼。但統是一個大原由體而達用從微而至著。

問一理之實而萬物分之以爲體故萬物各具一太極如此說則太極有分裂乎曰本只是一太極。而萬物各有禀受又自各全具一太極爾。如月在天只一而已。及散在江湖。則隨處而見。不可謂月分也。

eternal, the Air is also eternally united with it. From the time that Heaven and Earth existed, there was then this thing here revolving. A day has its own revolution; a month has its own revolution; and a year has its own revolution; this is just this thing revolving.

8. Before the Great Extreme moved, there was just Darkness; and in the midst of Darkness and Rest, spontaneously exists the root of the Light; in the midst of Light and Motion there is also the root of the Darkness. The reason why Rest necessarily follows Motion, is, because its root is in the Darkness; and the reason why Motion must succeed Rest, is, that its root is in the Light.

9. That the Great Extreme should have Motion and Rest, is the flowing forth of the heavenly decree (Fate). Some one doubting as to how Rest could be said to flow forth; he replied, that alternate Motion and Rest is what is meant by flowing forth. For example, can we not say that Autumn and Winter flow forth? If not, how could it be said that the Great Extreme "Rested and *generated* the Darkness?" This term ",generated" proves the point.

10. From the Great Extreme to the transmutation and production of the myriad of things, but one form includes the whole. It is not that this is prior, and that posterior; but, that they altogether constitute one Great Root, from *inertia* passing on to activity, from minuteness passing on to distinctness.

11. Being asked with regard to the substantiality of the one Fate, and its being divided amongst the myriad of things to pervade them, and hence each of the myriad of things having a Great Extreme within it: according to this, can the Great Extreme be divided into portions? He replied, as to Root, there is but one Great Extreme, and each of the myriad of things has received it, each

太極分開只是兩個陰陽。括盡了天下物事。

原極之所以得名。蓋取樞極之義聖人謂之太極者所以指夫天地萬物之根也周子因之而又謂之無極者。所以大無聲無臭之妙也。

太極無方所無形體無地位可頓放。若以未發時言之未發却只是靜。動靜陰陽皆只是形而下者然動亦太極之動。靜亦太極之靜。

但動靜非太極耳。故周子只以無極言之未發固不可謂之太極。然中含喜怒哀樂喜樂屬陽怒哀屬陰四者初未著而其理已具。若對已發言之容或可謂之太極然終是難說此皆只說得個髣髴形容當自體認。

動不是太極但動者太極之用耳。靜不是太極但靜者太極之體耳。

having within it an entire and complete Great Extreme: as, for example, the Moon in Heaven is but one, and when it is scattered amongst the rivers and canals, then it is seen in each; yet, we cannot say that the Moon is divided.

12. The Great Extreme opened out is just the two things Light and Darkness which enfold every thing in the Universe.

13. The Original Extreme derives its name from the idea of the highest pivot. The sages called it the Great Extreme, and thus pointed it out as the Root of Heaven, Earth, and all things. Hence Chow-tsze also designated it "The Infinite," and thus expressed its adorning immateriality. (Lit. without sound or scent).

14. The Great Extreme is not confined to place, has no bodily form, and no single place can contain it (*i. e.* it is Omnipresent, Incorporeal, and Infinite). If we speak of it before it was manifested forth, then, before manifestation was just its Rest. Motion and Rest, Darkness and Light, are all material things; but Motion, is the Motion of the Great Extreme, and Rest, is the Rest of the Great Extreme; yet, Motion and Rest are not the Great Extreme; and therefore, Chow-tsze designated it "The Infinite." Before manifestation it could not be called the Great Extreme, and yet, within it were Pleasure, Anger, Grief, and Joy; Pleasure and Joy pertain to the Light, Anger and Grief to the Darkness; and before these four were manifested forth, their Fate (*i. e.* ideas) already existed there. If we speak of these when manifested forth, then, I suppose, we may call them the Great Extreme; but, this is a difficult point to treat of; it is merely an attempt to illustrate the matter. You should investigate the subject minutely.

或問太極。曰。太極只是個極好至善底道理。人人有一太極。物物有一太極。周子所謂太極是天地人物萬善至好底表德。

才說太極。便帶著陰陽。才說性。便帶著氣。不帶著陰陽與氣。太極與性那裏收附。然要得分明。又不可不拆開說。

問先生說太極有是性。則有陰陽五行。此說性是如何。曰。想是某舊說。近思量又不然。此性字為稟於天者言。若太極只當說理。自是移易不得。易言一陰一陽之謂道。繼之者則謂之善。至於成之者方謂之性。此謂天所賦於人物。人物所受於天者也。

某嘗說太極是個藏頭底。動時屬陽。未動又屬陰了。

太極自是涵動靜之理。却不可以動靜分體用。蓋靜即太極之體也。動即太極之用也。譬如扇子只是一個扇子。動搖便是用。放下便是

15. Motion is not the Great Extreme, but that which has Motion is the active portion of the Great Extreme. Rest is not the Great Extreme, but that which has Rest is the inert portion of the Great Extreme.

16. One inquiring about the Great Extreme, he replied, the Great Extreme is just the best, and truly excellent, Principle. Each person and thing has a Great Extreme. What Chow-tsze means by the Great Extreme is the superlatively good, and most truly excellent manifested *virtus* of Heaven, Earth, Man, and all things.

17. When we speak of the "Great Extreme" we connect with it the Light and the Darkness; and when we speak of "Nature" we connect with it the Air. If these severally were not so connected with the Light and Darkness, and with the Air, then how could the Great Extreme and Nature be supported? Yet, when we wish to distinguish them clearly, we cannot but treat of them separately.

18. Being asked: You Sir, in speaking of the Great Extreme, said, that having Nature, then we have the Light and Darkness, and the Five Elements; what is this Nature? He replied, I suppose I said so on a former ococcasion, but now I do not think so. The designation "Nature" refers to our receiving this from Heaven; with regard to the Great Extreme, we ought to call it "Fate;" assuredly we must not change this designation. The Yih King states that "The alternating Light and Darkness is Reason. In causing these to revolve, it (*i. e.* Reason) is called The Good; and that which they complete, is called Nature." This is that which Heaven confers upon Men and things, and which Men and things receive from Heaven.

19. I have already said that the Great Extreme is one who hides his head: during motion it belongs to the Light, and when there is no motion, it belongs to the Darkness.

體才放下時便只是這一個道理及搖動時亦只是這一個道理。

梁文叔云太極兼動靜而言曰不是兼動靜太極有動靜喜怒哀樂未發也有個太極喜怒哀樂已發也有個太極只是一個太極流行於已發之際歛藏於未發之時。

或問太極曰未發便是理已發便是情。

太極者如屋之有極天之有極到這裏更沒法處理之極至者也陽動陰靜非太極動靜只是理有動靜理不可見因陰陽而後知理搭在陰陽上如人跨馬相似才生五行便被氣質拘定各爲一物。

亦各有一性而太極無不在也。

問劉子所謂天地之中卽周子所謂太極否曰只一般但名不同中。

只是恰好處書惟皇上帝降衷於下民亦只是恰好處極不是中。

20. The Great Extreme is in reality the Fate which contains Motion and Rest. We cannot take the Motion and Rest of the Great Extreme, and separate them from the active and inert portions of the Great Extreme; for Rest is the inactivity of the Great Extreme, and Motion is the activity of the Great Extreme. For example, a fan is but one fan; to fan oneself is the fan's activity, to lay it down is the fan's inactivity; but, when it is laid down, and when it is used in fanning, it is still the same fan.

21. Leang Wăn-sŭh said; the Great Extreme is connected with Motion and Rest. He replied: it is not connected with Motion and Rest. The Great Extreme *has* Motion and Rest. Before Pleasure, Anger, Grief, and Joy were manifested, the Great Extreme existed; and when these were manifested the Great Extreme was still in existence; this is but the one Great Extreme flowing forth to manifestation, and being hidden before manifestation.

22. One asking about the Great Extreme, he replied: Before it was manifested forth it was Fate; when manifested forth it is natural disposition; for example, "Moved and generated the Light," this statement shows natural disposition.

23. The Great Extreme resembles the highest summit of a house, and the highest point of Heaven; arrived at this point, there is no place beyond; it is the very extreme place of Fate. The Light moves and the Darkness rests, but the Great Extreme does not move or rest; it is merely that this Fate has Motion and Rest. Fate is invisible; its existence is known by the existence of the Light and the Darkness. Fate rests upon the Light and Darkness, as a man rides upon a horse. When the Five Elements are generated, then it becomes inherent in their

極之爲物。只是在中。如這燭臺中央簪處便是極。從這裏比到那裏也。恰好不曾加些。從那裏比到這裏也恰好不曾減些。

太極是個大底物事。四方上下曰宇。古往今來曰宙。無一個物似宙長遠。無一個物似宇樣大。四方去無極。上下去無極。是多少大。

瓦古瓦今往來不窮。自家心下須常認得這意思。問此是誰語。曰。此是古人語。象山常要說此語。但他說便只是這個又不用裏面許多節拍。却只守得個空蕩蕩底。公更看橫渠西銘初看有許多節拍。却是狹。充其量是甚麼樣大。

以理言之。則不可謂之有。以物言之。則不可謂之無。

或問康節云。道爲太極。又云心爲太極。道指天地萬物自然之理而言。心指人得是理以爲一身之主而言。曰固是。但太極只是個一

Aerial substance. Each Element is a separate thing, and each possesses a Nature inherent in it, and thus the Great Extreme is Omnipresent.

24. Being asked whether that which Lew-tsze calls the Centre of Heaven and Earth, is that which Chow-tsze designates the Great Extreme; he replied, yes: it is merely that the designations are different. "Chung" means the exact Centre. The phrase in the Shoo King, "Imperial *Shang-te* sends down the virtuous nature upon the people," just means this exact Centre. The extremity of a thing is not the Centre, but the extreme point of things is in the Centre. For instance, in this candlestick, the Centre, where the spike is, is just the extreme point; from this point to the outer rim, on all sides, the distance is the same without addition or diminution.

25. The Great Extreme is a great thing; its four quarters, Zenith and Nadir are called *Yu;* and duration from ancient to modern times is called *Tsow*. Nothing is so great as *Yu;* so great is it that the four quarters go into infinity; Zenith and Nadir also go into infinity. Nothing is so eternal as *Tsow;* from the most ancient times to the present, the coming and going of ages has been unceasing. Every one should be acquainted with this. Being asked who asserts this, he replied, the ancients state it; Seang-shan frequently does so, and what he states is just what I have said. He does not treat at any length about the inside, he only maintains its enormous cavity. You should diligently read Hwang-ken's Se Ming. At the first glance this book seems to contain numerous ideas on the subject, but the meaning is not very definite. If he had exerted his whole talent upon it, how valuable the book would have been!

26. Speaking with regard to Fate, we must not call

而無對者。

太極是五行陰陽之理皆有不是空底物事若是空時如釋氏說性相似。

極是道理之極至總天地萬物之理便是太極。

太極只是極至更無去處了至高至妙至精至神是沒去處濂溪恐人道太極有形故曰無極而太極是無之中有個極至之理。

問太極理也理如何動靜有形則有動靜太極無形恐不可以動靜言曰理有動靜故氣有動靜若理無動靜則氣何自而有動靜乎。

自見在事物而觀之則陰陽函太極推原其本則太極生陰陽。

問太極便是人心之至理曰事事物物皆有個極是道理之極至或曰如君之仁臣之敬便是極曰此是一事一物之極總天地萬物

(the Great Extreme) *Ens;* while, speaking with regard to Matter, we must not say that it is *non-Ens.**

27. Some one asked about the statements made by Kang-tsëĕ, that "Reason is the Great Extreme," and "Mind is the Great Extreme;" whether "Reason" here refers to the spontaneously existing Fate inherent in Heaven, Earth and all things: "Mind," to Man, obtaining this Fate to act as the Lord of the whole body? He replied, it is just so: but the Great Extreme is just One (*i.e.* unity) and without compare.

28. The Great Extreme is the Fate which exists in the Five Elements, in the Light and in the Darkness. It is not a mere abstraction: for, if it were, it would then resemble what the Buddhists call Nature.

29. The Extreme means the very extreme Principle. The Fate inherent in Heaven, Earth and all things, as one whole, is just the Great Extreme.

30. The Great Extreme is just the very extreme point beyond which we cannot go; most High, most Beautiful, most Subtile, most Divine; surpassing every thing. Lëen-khe, lest any one should imagine that the Great Extreme has bodily form, designates it "Infinite *and* Great Extreme;" that is, this extreme Fate is in the midst of *non-Ens* (*i. e.* Matter).

31. Being asked: The Great Extreme is Fate, how can Fate move and rest? That which has bodily form has Motion and Rest; but the Great Extreme is Incorporeal, and hence cannot, I suppose, be said to move and rest? He replied: Fate has (the power of) Motion and Rest, and therefore the Air has Motion and Rest; if Fate had not (the power of) Motion and Rest, then, how could the Air spontaneously have Motion and Rest?

---

* That is, it holds a middle place in the Kosmos.

之理。便是太極。太極本無此名。只是個表德。

太極如一本生上分為枝榦又分而生花生葉生生不窮到得成果子裏面又有生生無窮之理生將出去又是無限個太極更無停息只是到成果實時又却畧少歇也不是生到這裏自合少止所謂終始萬物莫盛乎艮艮止是生息之意

只是這一個物事所以萬物到秋冬時各自收斂閉藏忽然一下春來各自發越條暢這只是一氣一個消一個息只如人相似方其默時便是靜及其語時便是動那個滿山青黃碧綠無非是這太極。

所謂太極者不離乎陰陽而為言亦不雜乎陰陽而為言。

問萬物各具一太極此是以理言以氣言曰以理言

32. With regard to its manifestation in each matter and thing, then, the Light and Darkness enfold the Great Extreme; but, with regard to their origin, the Great Extreme generated the Light and Darkness.

33. Being asked with regard to the Great Extreme being the extreme Fate of Man's Mind, he replied: Every circumstance and every thing has an extreme; that is, the extreme point from which they spring. Some one observed, "Just as, for example, the Emperor's Benevolence, and the Minister's Respect, are extremes?" He replied, these are the extremes of each circumstance and thing; but, the Fate inherent in Heaven, Earth, and all things, as one whole, is the Great Extreme. The Great Extreme does not originally bear this designation; it is merely the manifested *virtus* which is so called.

34. The Great Extreme resembles a root which sprouts upwards, and divides into branches, and which also divides and produces blossoms and leaves, generating unceasingly. When the fruit is formed, then, it contains inside, the seed of endless generation, which generates, and springs forth. This is the Infinite Great Extreme, which never ceases altogether, but only when the fruit is perfected it ceases to generate for a while.* It is not that having generated to a certain point, then the One Whole (*i. e.* the Kosmos) must come to an end altogether. With regard to what is said respecting the beginning and ending of the myriad of things, viz., that they are perfected in the *Kăn* Diagram; this *Kăn* is cessation; that is, the cessation of generation.

35. It is solely owing to this (Great Extreme) that the myriad of things in Autumn and Winter are collected together and stored up, and that no sooner does Spring

---
* That is, when all things are about to return to chaos.

無極而太極。只是無形而有理周子恐人於太極之外更尋太極故以無極言之旣謂之無極則不可以有底道理强搜尋也問太極始於陽動乎曰陰靜是太極之本然陰靜又自陽動而生一靜一動便是一個闔闢自其闔闢之大者推而上之更無窮極不可以本始言。

問南軒云太極之體至靜。如何曰不是又云所謂至靜者貫乎已發未發而言如何曰如此却成一不正當尖斜太極。

天地之間只有動靜兩端循環不已更無餘事此之謂易而其動其靜則必有所以動靜之理是則所謂太極者也。

所謂太極者便只在陰陽裏所謂陰陽者便只在太極裏今人說是陰陽上別有一個無形無影裏是太極非也。

以上語類三十九條

return than each comes forth and expands. This is just the one Air alternately ceasing and again springing forth. This resembles a Man; when he is silent, then he is at Rest, and when he speaks, that is Motion. The Blue, Yellow, White, and Green colours which cover the hills are all owing to this Great Extreme.

36. That which is designated the Great Extreme, can neither be separated from, nor confounded with the Light and Darkness.

37. Being asked whether the statement that each thing has a Great Extreme inherent in it refers to Fate or to the Air; he replied, it refers to Fate.

38. The phrase "Infinite *and* Great Extreme," just means that Fate existed before bodily form. Chow-tsze, lest any one should seek a second Great Extreme beyond the true one, added the term "Infinite." Since he designates it "The Infinite," then we need not trouble ourselves to inquire whether it has form or not. Being asked whether the beginning of the Great Extreme is in the Light moving; he replied, the resting of the Darkness is the root of the Great Extreme, but the Rest of the Darkness is generated from the Motion of the Light. Alternate Motion and Rest is just alternate opening and shutting; and from the Great Opening and Shutting (of the Universe) upwards, is still more without limit or extreme. We cannot predicate commencement of the root.

39. Being asked with regard to the statement of Nan-hëen, that the *inertia* of the Great Extreme is extreme Rest, he replied; it is not so. Being further asked whether what is designated extreme Rest includes both manifestation and non-manifestation, he replied; if it did, then we should make an irregular or crooked Great Extreme, (*i.e.* not a perfect Circle).

性猶太極也。心猶陰陽也。太極只在陰陽之中非能離陰陽也。然至論太極則太極自是太極陰陽自是陰陽。惟性與心亦然。所謂一而二二而一也。_{以上三條出性理太極圖小註}

此道字即易之太極。一乃陽數之奇。二乃陰數之偶。三乃奇偶之積。其曰二生三者。猶所謂二與一爲三也。若直以一爲太極。則不容復言道生一矣。_{管程卷之}

動靜無端陰陽無始本不可以先後言。然就中間截斷言之。則亦不害其有先後也。觀周子所言太極動而生陽。則其未動之前固已嘗靜矣。又言靜極復動。則已靜之後固必有動矣。如春夏秋冬元亨利貞固不能無先後。然不冬則何以爲春。而不貞又何以爲元。

40. In the midst of Heaven and Earth are solely the two principles Motion and Rest revolving in a perpetual circle; there is nothing else besides these. This is designated "Change." This Motion and Rest must have a Fate which causes them, and this Fate is what is meant by the Great Extreme.

41. That which is designated the Great Extreme is in the Light and Darkness, and that which is designated Light and Darkness is in the Great Extreme. What some persons now assert about there being outside the Light and Darkness another formless and shadowless thing in which is the Great Extreme, is incorrect.

42. Nature resembles the Great Extreme, and Mind resembles the Light and Darkness. The Great Extreme is just in the midst of the Light and Darkness and cannot be separated from them; yet, to speak accurately of the Great Extreme, then, the Great Extreme is the Great Extreme, and the Light and Darkness are the Light and Darkness. Nature and Mind are also thus. This is what is meant by being "One, and yet Two; Two and yet One."

43. Reason is the Great Extreme of the Yih King. One, is the Light, the odd number; Two, is the Darkness, the even number; Three, is the odd and even numbers added together. When it is said that Two generated Three, this means that Two and One make Three. If we just consider Monad to be the Great Extreme, then we need not reiterate the statement that Reason generated Monad.

44. Motion and Rest have no beginning, the Light and Darkness have no commencement. As to orgin, we cannot predicate priority or posteriority of them; but if we divide them asunder in the middle, then we can do so without detriment. With regard to the statement of

就此看之又自有先後也。答王子合

前書所謂太極不在陰陽之外者正與來教所謂不倚於陰陽而生陰陽者合但某以形而上下者其名不可相雜故曰不在陰陽之中雖所自而言不同而初未嘗有異也。答程可久

太極之義正謂理之極致耳有是理即有是物無先後次序之可言。

故曰易有太極則是太極乃在陰陽之中而非在陰陽之外也今以大中訓之又以乾坤未判大衍未分之時論之恐未安也形而上者謂之道形而下者謂之器今論太極而曰其物謂之神又以天地未分元氣合而爲一者言之亦恐未安也。答程可久

Chow-tsze that the Great Extreme moved and generated the Light; then, before it moved it certainly was at rest. Also, when he says that it rested to the utmost limit, and again moved, then, after it had rested, it certainly had motion. For example, Spring, Summer Autumn and Winter; *Yuen, Háng, Le,* and *Ching;* these cannot but have priority and posteriority; for, if there was no Winter how could there be any Spring; and if there was no Ching, how could there be any Yuen? If we regard the matter thus, assuredly there is priority and posteriority.

45. What the former letter states about the great Extreme not being outside the Light and Darkness, is the same as what the present communication says, viz., that independently of the Light and Darkness, it generated the Light and Darkness. I however consider that the terms "Corporeal" and "Incorporeal" mean that these must never be confounded together. Hence I said that the Great Extreme is in the centre of the Light and Darkness. You Sir, also consider that the terms "Corporeal" and "Incorporeal" mean that they must not be confounded together, and hence you say that the great Extreme is not outside the Light and Darkness. Although our modes of expression are different, yet there is no difference whatever as to meaning.

46. The Great Extreme just means the Extreme Fate. Fate existing then Matter exists; we cannot predicate priority or posteriority, first or second, concerning them. The Yih King says, "Change has the Great Extreme," that is, the Great Extreme is in the centre of the Light and Darkness, and is not outside them. Now to assert that it is the Great Centre, or to speak of it before *Kheen* and *Khwán* divided, and the Great Extension (*i. e.* Number) commenced, I fear, is not correct. That which

太極含動靜則可以本體而言也謂太極有動靜則可以流行而言也若謂太極便是動靜則是形而上下者不可分而易有太極之言亦贅矣。答楊子直

太極乃兩儀四象八卦之理不可謂無但未有形象之可言爾故自此而生一陰一陽乃為兩儀而四象八卦又是從此生皆有自然次第不由人力安排然自孔子以來亦無一人見得至邵康節後明其說極有條理意趣可玩恐未可忽更詳之。答林黃中

未發者太極之靜已發者太極之動。答呂子約

銖問極之為言究竟至極不可有加之謂以狀此理之名義則舉天下無以加此之稱也故常在物之中為物之的物無之則無以為

is Incorporeal is Reason, and that which is Corporeal is the Receptacle. Now, in speaking of the Great Extreme to say that its Matter is designated God; or, to speak of it before Heaven and Earth were divided, when the Original Air was chaotic and one, I also fear is not correct.

47. We may say that the Great Extreme enfolds Motion and Rest; this refers to its original body. We may also say that the Great Extreme has Motion and Rest; this refers to its flowing forth and pervading. If we say that the Great Extreme is merely Motion and Rest, then we do not discriminate between the Corporeal and the Incorporeal, and the statement that "Change has the Great Extreme" is verbose.

48. The Great Extreme is the Fate inherent in the two E, the Four Simulacra, and the Eight Diagrams. We cannot say that it has no existence, and yet, we must not ascribe corporeal form to it. Therefore the Light and Darkness which are generated from this, are the Two E; and the Four Simulacra and Eight Diagrams which are generated from it, have their order spontaneously, and are not arranged by human power. But, from the time of Confucius no one understood this until Shaou Kang-tsëĕ afterwards explained it. His treatise is most connected and interesting; it should be carefully studied and not hastily run over.

49. Non-manifestation is the Rest of the Great Extreme; and manifestation is the Motion of the Great Extreme.

50. Shoo asked the meaning of the term "Extreme." Is it the very utmost extreme, so that nothing can be added to it, which is signified by this appellation of Fate? That is to say, is it the appellation to which nothing in the whole world can be added? Is this the reason why it is always in the centre of things, being their central

根主而不能以有立故以爲在中之義則可而便訓極爲中則不可以有形者論之則如屋之有脊棟囷廩之有通天柱常在此物之中央四面八方望之以取正千條萬別本之以有生禮所謂民極詩所謂四方之極其義一也未知推說如此是否曰是 答董叔重〇以上文集八條

THE GREAT EXTREME. 51

point; and that whatever has not got this, then, that thing has nothing which can be regarded as the source of the governing power, and cannot have any existence. Therefore we can consider this to be *in* the centre of things, yet, we must not say that the Extreme of a thing *is* the centre. To illustrate this by what has form, then, it resembles the topmost beam of a house, or the supporting pillar in a granary, which are always in the centre of these buildings, the four sides and eight divisions looking towards them when properly adjusted. Innumerable branches spring from this Root. The people's Extreme of the Le King, and the Extreme of the four quarters of the She King, have precisely the same meaning; is all this correct or not? He replied, yes.

天地

天地初閒只是陰陽之氣。這一個氣運行。磨來磨去。磨得急了。便楞許多渣滓。裏面無處出便結成個地在中央。氣之清者便為天。為日月。為星辰。只在外常周環運轉。地便在中央不動。不是在下。

天運不息。晝夜輥轉故地榷在中間。便天有一息之停則地須陷下。惟天運轉之急故凝結得許多渣滓在中間。地者氣之渣滓也所以道輕清者為天重濁者為地。

問天有形質否。曰只是個旋風下頓上堅。道家謂之剛風。人常說天有九重分九處為號。非也只是旋有九耳。但下面氣較濁而暗上面至高處則至清至明耳。

天地始初混沌未分時想只有水火二者水之滓腳便成地今登高

PART III.

HEAVEN AND EARTH.

1. In the beginning Heaven and Earth were just the Light and Dark Air. This one Air revolved grinding round and round. When it ground quickly much sediment was compressed, which having no means of exit, coagulated and formed the Earth in the centre. The subtile portion of the Air then became Heaven, and the Sun, Moon, and Stars, which unceasingly revolve on the outside. The Earth is in the centre and is motionless, it is not below the centre.

2. Heaven revolving without ceasing, Day and Night also revolve, and hence the Earth is exactly in the centre. If Heaven should stand still for one moment, then the Earth must fall down; but, Heaven revolves quickly and hence much sediment is coagulated in the centre. The Earth is the sediment of the Air; and hence it is said that the light and pure Air became Heaven, the heavy and muddy Air became Earth.

3. Being asked whether Heaven has any bodily substance; he replied: It is just a spiral wind, soft below and hard above: the Taouists designate it "a hard wind." It is frequently asserted that Heaven has nine separate spheres, and designations are given to these as being nine separate places. This is erroneous; the spiral ascent* has just nine (spheres). The lower portion of the Air is gross and dark, while the highest part of the upper portion is most pure and most bright.

4. At the beginning of Heaven and Earth, before chaos was divided, I think there were only two things, Fire and

---

* Thus, ◉; not, ◉. See 五經類編.

而望羣山皆為波浪之狀。便是水泛如此。只不知因甚麼時凝了。
初間極輭後來方凝得硬。問想得如潮水湧起沙相似。曰然。水之極濁便成地火之極清便成風霆雷電日星之屬。
問自開闢以來至今未萬年不知已前如何。曰已前亦須如此一番明白來又問天地會壞否曰不會壞只是相將人無道極了便一齊打合混沌一番。人物都盡又重新起又問生第一個人時如何。
曰以氣化二五之精合而成形釋家謂之化生如今物之化生者甚多如虱然。
方渾淪未判陰陽之氣混合幽暗及其既分中間放得開闊光朗。而兩儀始立邵康節以十二萬九千六百年為一元。則是十二萬九千六百年之前又是一個大開闢更以上亦復如此直是動靜無

Water: and the sediment of the Water formed the Earth. When we ascend a height and look down, the host of hills resemble the waves of the sea in appearance; the Water just flowed like this: I know not at what period it coagulated. At first it was very soft, but afterwards it coagulated and became hard. One asked whether it resembled sand thrown up by the tide? He replied, just so: the coarsest sediment of the Water became the Earth, and the most pure portion of the Fire became Wind, Thunder, Lightning, Sun, and Stars.

5. Being asked: From the commencement of Heaven and Earth to the present time is not 10,000 years; I know not how it was before that time? He replied, Before that there was another clear opening, (*i.e.* another Heaven and Earth) like the present one. Being further asked whether Heaven and Earth can perish altogether; he replied, They cannot: but, when mankind totally degenerate, then the whole shall return to Chaos, and Men and things shall all cease to exist; and then the world shall begin again. Some one asked how the First Man was generated; and he replied: By the transmutation of the Air; the subtile portions of the Light and Darkness and the Five Elements, united and produced his form. The Buddhists call this transmuting and generating. At present things are transmuted and generated in abundance like lice.

6. Before Chaos was divided the Light-Dark Air was mixed up and dark, and when it divided, the centre formed an enormous and most brilliant opening, and the Two E were established. Shaou Kang-tseĕ considers 129,600 years to be a Yuen (Kalpa); then, before this period of 129,600 years there was another opening and spreading out of the world; and before that again, there was another like the present; so that, Motion and Rest,

陰陽無始。小者大之影只晝夜便可見五峯所謂一氣大息震盪無垠。海宇變動山勃川湮人物消盡舊迹大滅是謂鴻荒之世。嘗見高山有螺蚌殼。或生石中此石即舊日之土螺蚌即水中之物下者却變而爲高柔者却變而爲剛此事思之至深有可驗者問天地未判時下面許多都已有否曰只是都有此理天地生物千萬年古今只不離許多物
地却是有空缺處天却四方上下都周匝無空缺。逼塞滿皆是天地之四向底下却靠著那天天包地其氣無不通恁地看來渾只是天了。氣却從地中迸出又見地廣處。
天包乎地天之氣又行乎地之中故橫渠云。地對天不過。
問天地之所以高深曰天只是氣非獨是高只今人在地上便只見

Light and Darkness, have no beginning. As little things shadow forth great things, this may be illustrated by the revolutions of Day and Night. What Woo-fung says about the Great Cessation of the entire Air, the vast and boundless agitation of all things, the whole expanse of waters changing position, the mountains bursting asunder, the channels being obliterated, Men and things all coming to an end, and the ancient vestages all destroyed—all this refers to the utter destruction of the world by Deluge We frequently see, on lofty mountains, the shells of the sea-snail and pearl-oyster, as it were generated in the middle of stones; these stones were (part of) the soil of the former world. The sea-snail and pearl-oyster belong to the water; so that, that which was below, changed and became high; that which was soft, changed and became hard. This is a deep subject, and should be investigated.

7. Being asked whether the multitude of things existed before Heaven and Earth divided; he replied: There was merely the idea of each thing. Heaven and Earth generate all things, and throughout all time, ancient, and modern, cannot be separated from all things.

8. The Earth has hollow places. Heaven completely surrounds it on all sides, above and below, and has no hollow place. Heaven presses in and fills up every place. The four quarters of Earth decline downwards and rest upon Heaven. Heaven embraces Earth, and his Air penetrates every part, so that the whole is Heaven. The Air is scattered forth from the interior of the Earth, and thus is seen Earth's wide capacity.

9. Heaven embraces Earth, and his Air flows into Earth; hence Hwang-keu says, Earth cannot be compared to Heaven.

如此高要之連地下亦是天又云世間無一個物事大故地恁地

大地只是氣之渣滓故厚而深也。

天地但陰陽之一物依舊是陰陽之氣所生也。

康節言天依形地附氣所以重複而言不出此意者惟恐人於天地之外別尋去處故也天地無外所以其形有涯而其氣無涯也為

其氣極緊故能扛得地住不然則墜矣氣外更須有軀殼甚厚所

以固此氣也若夫地動只是一處動亦不至遠也。

古今曆家只是推得個陰陽消長界分爾如何得似康節說得那天

依地地附天天地自相依附天依形地附氣底幾句。

問天依形地附氣曰恐人道下面有物天行急地閣在中。

天明則日月不明天無明夜半黑淬淬地天之正色。

10. Being asked about the height and depth of Heaven and Earth; he replied: Heaven is merely Air; not only is it so high overhead as it now appears to men on Earth, but we should be aware that the portion beneath the Earth is also Heaven. He also said: because there is nothing else in the world which can be considered so large, therefore, the size of the Earth is exaggerated. The Earth is just the sediment of the Air, and hence it is dense and deep.

11. Heaven and Earth are but one Light-Dark thing, originally generated by the Light-Dark Air.

12. Kang-tsëĕ says, that Heaven rests upon form, and Earth reclines upon Air. The reason why he frequently repeats this, and does not deviate fron the idea, is, lest people should seek some other place beyond Heaven and Earth. There is nothing outside Heaven and Earth, and hence their form has limits, while their Air has no limit. Because the Air is extremely condensed, therefore it can support the Earth; if it were not so, the Earth would fall down. Outside the Air there must also be a most thick shell by which it is strengthened. With regard to Earthquakes, only one place is agitated at a time, and this does not extend to any great distance.

13. Ancient and modern Astronomers merely arranged the limits of the decrease and fulness of the Light and Darkness; how could they, as Kang-tsëĕ does, assert that Heaven rests upon Earth, and Earth leans upon Heaven; that Heaven and Earth mutually rest and lean upon each other; and that Heaven rests upon form, and Earth leans upon Air?

14. Being asked why it is said that Heaven rests upon form, and Earth leans upon Air; he replied, lest men should assert that there was any thing beneath them.

天只是一個大底物須是大著心腸看他始得以天運言之一日固是轉一匝然又有大轉底時候不可如此偏滯求也

天轉也非自東而西也非旋環磨轉却是側轉

問康節論六合之外恐無外否曰理無內外六合之形須有內外日從東畔升西畔沈明日又從東畔升這上面許多下面亦許多豈不是六合之內曆家算氣只算得到日月星辰運行處上去更算不得安得是無內外

問天地之心亦靈否還只是漠然無爲曰天地之心不可道是不靈但不如人恁地思慮伊川曰天地無心而成化聖人有心而無爲

問天地之心天地之理理是道理心是主宰底意否曰心固是主宰

Heaven revolves quickly, and Earth is placed in the centre.

15. If Heaven were bright, then the Sun and Moon could not give any light; but, Heaven is not bright, the darkness of midnight is the real colour of Heaven.

16. Heaven is just a great thing; we should enlarge our ideas in order to contemplate it intelligently. With regard to Heaven's revolutions, he makes one revolution each day; but, he has besides, periods of Great Revolutions which cannot be determined with the same accuracy.

17. Heaven's revolutions are not from East to West, nor horizontally like a millstone when grinding, but it revolves obliquely.

18. Being asked: Kang-tsëĕ speaks of the outside of the six points,* but I suppose there is no outside? He replied, Fate (*i. e.* the Vacuum) has no outside nor inside; but the form (*i. e.* the Air) of the six points must have inside and outside. The Sun rises in the East and sets in the West, and to-morrow it will rise again in the East; he travels as much space above as below; is not this within the six points? Astronomers in calculating the movements of the Air, only calculate the revolutions of the Sun, Moon, and Stars; their calculations cannot extend beyond these; how then should they know that there is no inside or outside?

19. Being asked whether the Mind of Heaven and Earth is spiritual, or merely devoid of thought and passive; he replied, We must not assert that the Mind of Heaven and Earth is not spiritual; but, it does not think or concern itself about matters like Man. E-chuen says, that Heaven and Earth without exerting Mind make and transmute; the Sage exerts Mind but is passive.

* North, South, East, West, Zenith and Nadir.

底意。然所謂主宰者卽是理也。不是心外別有個理。理外別有個心。又問此心字與帝字相似否曰人字似天字心字似帝字。問天地無心仁便是天地之心若使其有心必有思慮營爲天地曷嘗有思慮來然其所以四時行。百物生者蓋以其合當如此。便如此不待思維此所以爲天地之道曰如此則易所謂復其見天地之心正大而天地之情可見又如何所說祇說得他無心處。耳若果無心則須牛生出馬桃樹上發李花他又却自定程子曰以主宰謂之帝以性情謂之乾他這名義自定心便是他個主宰處。所以謂天地以生物爲心。天地別無勾當只是以生物爲心。一元之氣運轉流通略無停間。只

20. Being asked about the Mind of Heaven and Earth, and the Fate of Heaven and Earth ; whether Fate is the Virtuous Nature, and Mind the Ruling Power? He replied, Mind certainly is the Ruling Power, but that which constitutes him the Ruling Power is Fate. Not that apart from Mind their exists this Fate, or apart from Fate there exists this Mind (*i. e.* the two are eternally united together). Being further asked whether Mind and the (Supreme) Emperor are the same, he replied, Man is the same as Heaven, and Mind is the same as the (Supreme) Emperor (*i. e. Shang-te*).

21. Being asked with regard to Heaven and Earth not exercising Mind ; and, Benevolence being the Mind of Heaven and Earth. If they possess Mind, then they must think and devise and plan ; yet, how can Heaven and Earth thus plan and devise ? Moreover, that by which the Four Seasons revolve and all things are generated, is that since these things ought to be so, therefore they are so, and do not wait for devising and calculating : is this the way of Heaven and Earth ? He replied, just so ; then what the Yih King says as to the Fŭh Diagram manifesting forth the Mind of Heaven and Earth is strictly correct, and the natural disposition of Heaven and Earth can thus be seen. Moreover how, according to what you have just said, can you only speak of their *not* exercising Mind (*i. e.* at certain times they do exercise Mind, and at certain periods they do not). If in reality they never exercised Mind, then assuredly oxen would produce horses, and peach trees would send forth plum blossoms. But their course is spontaneously determined. Chang-tsze says, "Because of the Ruling Power he (*i. e.* Heaven) is called the (Supreme) Emperor, because of his nature he is called Khëen (hard)." These his appel-

是生出許多萬物而已問程子謂天地無心而成化聖人有心而
無爲曰這是說天地無心處且如四時行百物生天地何所容心。
至於聖人則順理而已復何爲哉所以明道云天地之常以其心
普萬物而無心聖人之常以其情順萬事而無情說得最好問普
萬物莫是以心周偏而無私否曰天地以此心普及萬物人得之
遂爲人之心物得之遂爲物之心草木禽獸接著遂爲草木禽獸
之心只是一個天地之心爾今須要知得他有心處又要見得他
無心處只恁定說不得。
萬物生長是天地無心時枯槁欲生是天地有心時。
造化之運如磨上面常轉而不止萬物之生似磨中撒出有粗有細。

lations mean "spontaneously determined." Mind is just their Ruling Power, and hence it is said that Heaven and Earth exert their Mind in generating things.

22. Heaven and Earth have no other occupation than merely to exercise Mind in generating things. The one original Air revolves, flows forth, and pervades, without the least cessation, merely generating the myriad of things and nothing more. Being asked as to the statement of Ching-tsze that "Heaven and Earth without exerting Mind make and transmute, the Sage exerts Mind but is passive," he replied: This refers to the period during which Heaven and Earth do not exert Mind. For, when the Four Seasons are revolving, and all things are generated, why should Heaven and Earth then exert Mind? With regard to the Sage, he merely obeys Fate, and nothing more; what further has he to do? Hence Ming-taou says, that "the invariable rule of Heaven and Earth is to exhaust their Mind by pervading all things with it, and the Sage's invariable rule is to exhaust his natural disposition by adapting it to all circumstances." This is an excellent statement. Being asked whether the pervading all things means thoroughly pervading all things by their Mind without partiality, he replied: Heaven and Earth with this Mind pervade the Myriad of things; Man obtains it, and then it is the Mind of Man; Things obtain it, and then it is the Mind of Things; Grass, Trees, Birds, and Beasts obtain it, and then it is the Mind of Grass, Trees, Birds and Beasts; this is just the one Mind of Heaven and Earth. You should now understand what is meant by their exerting Mind, and also perceive the meaning of their not exerting Mind; only we must not assert the one to the exclusion of the other.

自是不齊。又曰。天地之形如人以兩椀相合貯水於內以手常常掉開則水在內不出稍住手則水漏矣。天在四畔地居其中減得一尺地遂有一尺氣但人不見耳。此是未成形者。及至浮而上降而下則已成形者。若融結糟粕煨燼卽是氣之渣滓。要之皆是示人以理。晝夜運而無息便是陰陽之兩端其四邊散出紛擾者便是游氣以生人物之萬殊。如麵磨相似其四邊只管層層散出天地之氣運轉無已只管層層生出人物。其中有粗有細如人物有偏有正。

帝是理爲主。

蒼蒼之謂天。運轉周流不已。便是那個。而今說天有個人在那裏批

23. When the myriad of things are generated and flourishing, that is the period when Heaven and Earth do not exert their Mind: but, when all things have decayed away, and require to be again generated, that is the time when Heaven and Earth exert their Mind.

24. The circle of formation and transmutation, resembles the top stone of a mill constantly turning round without cessation; and the generation of the myriad of things resembles the grain scattered about from the centre of the mill, which is both coarse and fine, and is not all alike. He also said, the form of Heaven and Earth, is as if one should take two bowls and fit them together (one inverted over the other), storing up water in the inside. While the hands are kept in constant motion, the water remains within and does not escape; but, if the hands stop for a moment, then the water leaks out.

25. Heaven is on the four sides, while Earth is stationary in the midst. Wherever a foot of Earth is wanting, there is a foot of Air to fill up the cavity; yet men perceive it not. This is before their form is completed. When Heaven floats and ascends, and Earth sinks down, then their form is completed. With regard to coagulating, and dregs, and residue; these refer to the sediment of the Air, and in fact these terms are all used for the instruction of mankind.

26. Day and Night revolve without ceasing, and are just the two Principles Light and Darkness. That which is confusedly scattered forth on their four sides is just the dispersed Air from which the myriad of differing Men and things are generated: they resemble a flour mill, the four sides continually, scattering forth layers. The Air of Heaven and Earth revolves without ceasing, continually generating both Men and things in layers; in their

判罪惡固不可說道全無主之者又不可這裏要人見得。

問經傳中天字曰要人自看得分曉也有說蒼蒼者也有說主宰者也有單訓理時。

天以氣而依地之形地以形而附天之氣天包乎地地特天中之一物爾天以氣而運乎外故地㩴在中間隤然不動使天之運有一息停則地須陷下。

季通云地上便是天。

天地不恕謂蕭殺之類。

問天有形質否曰無只是氣旋轉得緊如急風然至上面極高處轉得愈緊若轉纔慢則地便脫墜矣。

道家有高處有萬里剛風之說便是那裏氣清緊低處則氣濁故緩

midst is fine and coarse Air, as Men and things are depraved and upright.

27. The (Supreme) Emperor* is Fate acting as Lord.

28. The Azure Sky is Heaven; it is just this which revolves and flows forth without cessation. Now, to say that Heaven has a person up there who judges good and evil, we must not assert this. To say that there is nothing whatever which rules it, we also must not assert. People should know this.

29. Being asked the meaning of the word "Heaven" in the Classics, he replied, people must observe and clearly distinguish for themselves. In some places the Azure Sky is meant, in others the Ruling Power, and in others Fate is meant.

30. Heaven by his Air rests upon Earth's form; and Earth by her form, leans upon Heaven's Air. Heaven embraces Earth, and Earth is but a thing in the midst of Heaven. Heaven by his Air revolves outside, and hence Earth is, in fact, in his midst, steady and without motion. If Heaven should cease to revolve for one moment, then Earth must fall down.

31. Ke-tung says, that all above the Earth is just Heaven.

32. That "Heaven and Earth will not forgive," means that all things are doomed to destruction.

33. Being asked whether Heaven has bodily substance, he replied, no; it is merely Air which revolves compactly, like a whirlwind. At the top, the highest place, it revolves still more compactly; if it revolved more slowly, then Earth would fall down.

34. The Taouists say that at the highest point of

---

* 上帝, the Emperor of Gods and Men: the First Ancestor of the human race.

散想得高山更上去立人不住了那裏氣又緊故也離騷有九天
之說注家妄解云有九天據某觀之只是九重盖天運行有許多
重數裏面重數較軟至外面則漸硬想到第九重只成硬殼相似。
那裏轉得又愈緊矣。
生物之初陰陽之精自凝結成兩個盖是氣化而生如虱子自然爆
出來旣有此兩個一牝一牡後來却從種子漸漸生去便是以形
化萬物皆然。
天地形而下者乾坤形而上者天地乾坤之形殼乾坤天地之性情
夫乾其靜也專其動也直是以大生焉夫坤其靜也翕其動也闢是
以廣生焉本義云乾一而實故以質言而曰大坤二而虛故以量
言而曰廣學者不曉請問曰此兩句解得極分曉盖言以形言之

Heaven, there is an infinite hard wind.* It is merely that in that place the Air is pure and compressed. The lower part of Heaven is just the dregs of the Air, and there it revolves slowly and loosely. I suppose that if we could ascend above the highest mountains we could not stand, because the Air is so condensed there. The Le Saou speaks of nine Heavens, and the Commentators incorrectly explain this to mean that there are nine different Heavens. I consider that Heaven has nine spheres. Heaven revolving has several spheres; the inside of each is soft and becomes gradually hard towards the outside. I think that at the ninth sphere there is a hard shell, as it were, formed; and at that place it revolves still more compactly.

35. At the beginning of the generation of things, the subtile portion of the Light and Darkness spontaneously coagulated and formed two (of each species): this is the Air transmuting and generating like lice. These two spontaneously burst asunder, and when they existed as a male and a female, then, generation afterwards took place by degrees from this seed. This is form transmuting; the myriad of things are generated thus.

36. Heaven and Earth are corporeal, *Khëen-khwǎn* (Light and Darkness) are incorporeal: Heaven and Earth are the body of *Khëen-khwǎn*, and *Khëen-khwǎn* are the nature of Heaven and Earth.

37. "Now *Khëen's* Rest is undivided attention; his Motion is straight forward; and he is the Great Generator. With regard to Earth, her Rest is closing together; her Motion is opening; and she is the Capacious Generatrix." The Pun-e says, *Khëen* is Monad and is solid; and hence, speaking with regard to substance, he is called "Great." *Khwǎn* is Duality, and is hollow; and hence, speaking

---

* *Lit:* 10,000 *li.*

則天包地外地在天中所以說天之質大以理與氣言之則地却
包著天天之氣却盡在地之中地盡承受那天之氣所以說地之
量廣大只是一個物事一故實從裏面便實出來流行發生只是
一個物事所以說乾一而實地雖是堅然却虛所以天之氣流行
乎地之中皆從地裏發出來所以說坤二而虛用之云.地形如肺
形質雖硬而中本虛故陽氣升降乎其中無所障礙雖金石也透
過去.地便承受得這氣發育萬物日然要之天形如一個鼓鞴天
便是那鼓鞴外面皮殼子中間包得許多氣開闔消長所以說乾
一而實.地只是個物事中間盡是這氣升降往來緣中間虛故容
得這升降往來以其包得地所以說其質之大以其容得天之氣
所以說其量之廣非是說地之形有盡故以量言也只是說地盡

HEAVEN AND EARTH.   73

with regard to her capability of containing, she is called "Capacious." His pupils, not understanding, asked for further explanation. He replied: The meaning of these two statements is perfectly clear. Speaking with regard to their form, then Heaven embraces Earth on the outside, and Earth is in the midst of Heaven; hence it is said that his substance is "Great." Speaking with regard to Fate inherent in Air (*i. e.* Chaos), then Earth embraces Heaven, and Heaven's Air is all in the midst of the Earth. Earth receives his entire Air, and hence her capability of containing is designated "Capacious." "Great" is just oneness; he is Monad, and therefore solid; from the inside to the outside he is all substantial, flowing forth, and generating. He is just one thing, and hence it is said that *Khëen* is Monad and substantial. Earth, although she is firm, is yet hollow; and therefore Heaven's Air flows forth into the midst of Earth, and issues forth from the interior of the Earth; hence it is said that *Khwăn* is Duad and hollow. Yung-tsze said, the form of the Earth resembles the lungs; although the substance is hard, yet the centre is hollow, and hence the subtile Air ascends and descends in her midst, and there is no obstruction. Although metal and stones can pass through, yet, Earth receives this Air, and generates and nourishes the myriad of things? He replied; Just so; in fact Heaven's form is like a bellows; Heaven is just the outer skin case of the bellows; in the centre it encloses much Air, opening out (into the formed universe) and shutting up (in Chaos), increasing and diminishing; and hence it is said that *Khëen* is Monad and solid. Earth is but matter; her midst is full of this Air ascending and descending, coming and going. Because her centre is hollow, therefore she can contain this ascending and descending,

容得天之氣。所以說其量之廣爾。

或問伊川說以主宰謂之帝。孰爲主宰。曰自有主宰。蓋天是個至剛至陽之物。自然如此運轉不息。所以如此。必有爲之主宰者。這樣處。要人自見得。非言語所能盡也。因舉莊子孰綱維是孰主張是十數句。曰他也見得這道理。

列子曰天積氣。日月星宿亦積氣中之有光耀者。此言得之。或問天地壞也不壞。曰旣有形氣。如何得不壞。但一個壞了便有一個生得來。以上語類三十九條

問康節天地自相依附之說。燼以爲此說與周子太極圖程子動靜無端陰陽無始之義一致。非曆家所能窺測。曰康節之言大體固如是矣。然曆家之說亦須考之方見其細密處。如禮記月令疏。及

coming and going Air. Because he embraces Earth, hence it is said that his substance is "Great;" because she contains Heaven's Air, hence it is said that her "Capacity" is great. It is not because Earth's form is complete that "Capaciousness" is predicated of her; but, because Earth receives the entire of Heaven's Air,* therefore we speak of the vastness of her "Capacity."

38. Some one asked, with reference to E-chuen's statement that the governing Power is called the "Ruler" (Shang-te); what is the governing power? He replied there certainly is a governing power. Heaven is a most hard and *Yang* thing, spontaneously revolving without ceasing. There must be a governing power, which causes this Motion. People must inquire into this matter for themselves; it cannot be fully decided by merely discoursing about it. Then, pointing out Chang-tsze's several statements as to what regulates and directs all this, he said: He also understands this matter.

39. Lĕe-tsze says, Heaven is accumulated Air; the Sun, Moon, and Stars, are lights in the midst of this accumulated Air. This is correct. Some one asking whether Heaven and Earth are perishable or not? He replied, Since they have body and Air (*i. e.* soul), how can they avoid perishing? But, after each destruction, there is a fresh generation.

40. Being asked about Kang-tsĕĕ's statement, that "Heaven and Earth mutually lean upon each other;" whether this statement does not accord with Chow-tsze's diagram of the Great Extreme, with Chang-tsze's statement that Motion and Rest have no beginning, Light and Darkness have no commencement, and does not depend upon the observations of Astronomers? He replied: That

---

* Cicero says, "*Terra semen sparsum excipit.*"

晉天文志。皆不可不讀也。答李敬子

問清濁。以氣言。剛柔美惡。以氣之爲質言。清濁恐屬天。剛柔美惡恐屬地。曰陳了翁云天氣而地質前輩已有此說矣。答徐彥章

天地之間。品物萬形。各有所事。惟天確然於上。地隤然於下。一無所爲。只以生物爲事。故易曰天地之大德曰生。而程子亦曰。天只是以生爲道。其論復見天地之心。又以動之端言之。其理亦已明矣。然所謂以生爲道者。亦非謂將生來做道也。答張欽夫

康節所著漁樵對問。論天地自相依附。形有涯而氣無涯。極有條理。當時想是如此說。故伊川然之。答呂伯恭〇以上文集四條

is the substance of what Kang-tsëĕ says ; but, the statements of Astronomers should also be examined into, and then you can understand the matter minutely. For example, the Yue-lin-soo of the Le Ke, with the T'ëen-wăn-che of the Tsin Dynasty ; you must not omit studying these works.

41. Being asked: The designations "clear and muddy" refer to the Air; "Hard and Soft," beautiful and ugly, refer to the Air as substance; I suppose the "clear and muddy" pertain to Heaven, the "Hard and Soft," beautiful and ugly, pertain to Earth? He replied ; Chin Leaouung says, Heaven is Air ; Earth is substance. The ancients assert this.

42. In the midst of Heaven and Earth, the various classes of things have a myriad different forms ; and each has its own sphere of action. But, Heaven is steadily fixed above and Earth is humbly placed below, and they do not perform a single act except generating things. Hence the Yih King says, "The great *virtus* of Heaven and Earth is called generating ;" and Ching-tsze also says, that the path of Heaven is merely to generate. This refers to the Fŭh Diagram which manifests the Mind of Heaven and Earth : also, if referred to the commencement of Motion, this doctrine is clear. But, when he uses the phrase "Take generating to be Taou," he does not mean to assert that living things are Taou *(Reason)*.

43. Kang-tsëĕ in his Dialogue between the Fisherman and the Woodman states that Heaven and Earth mutually lean upon each other, their form being finite, but their Air infinite ; this statement is excellent. At that time, I suppose, the matter was so stated, and hence E-chuen's idea agrees with this.

陰陽　五行　時令

天地統是一個大陰陽。一年又有一年之陰陽。一月又有一月之陰陽。一日一時皆然。以下論陰陽

陰陽五行之理須常常看得在目前則自然牢固矣。

五行相為陰陽又各自為陰陽。

得五行之秀者為人只說五行而不言陰陽者盡做這人須是五行方做得成然陰陽便在五行中所以周子云五行一陰陽也舍五行無別討陰陽處。如甲乙屬木甲便是陽。乙便是陰。丙丁屬火丙便是陽丁便是陰。不須更說陰陽而陰陽在其中矣。或曰如言四時而不言寒暑耳曰然。

陽無驟生之理。如冬至前半月。中氣是小雪陽已生三十分之一分。

PART IV.
LIGHT AND DARKNESS.—THE FIVE ELEMENTS.—THE SEASONS.

1. Heaven and Earth as one whole are a great Light and Darkness; each year has a year's Light and Darkness; each month has a month's Light and Darkness; each day and each hour are thus.

2. The doctrine of the Light and Darkness, and the Five Elements, must always be made the subject of ocular demonstration, and then it will be firmly remembered.

3. The Five Elements placed in opposition are Light and Darkness, and each one is in itself both Light and Darkness.

4. Man obtains the subtile portion of the Five elements. The Five Elements are merely mentioned, and not Light and Darkness, because in making Man, it is the Five Elements which form him, but the Light and Darkness are just in the midst of the Five Elements. Hence Chowtsze says, that the Five Elements are one Light and Darkness. Casting away the Five Elements, then there is no other place where the Light and Darkness are to be found. For instance, Këa and Yih (two Astronomical characters) belong to Wood; Këa is Light and Yih is Darkness. Ping and Ting belong to Fire; Ping is Light and Ting is Darkness. We must not speak of the Light and Darkness separately from the Five Elements, for the Light and Darkness are in their midst. Some one observing that to do so would be like speaking of the Four Seasons without mentioning Heat and Cold; he replied, Just so.

5. The Light does not generate rapidly; as, for instance, in the first half of the month of the winter sols-

到得冬至前幾日。須已生到二十七八分。到是日方始成一畫不是昨日全無今日一旦便都復了。大抵剝盡處便生莊子云造化密移疇覺之哉這語自說得好又如列子亦謂運轉無已天地密移疇覺之哉凡一氣不頓進一形不頓虧亦不覺其成不覺其虧。
蓋陰陽浸消浸盛人之一身自少至老亦莫不然。
天地間只有一個陰陽。故程先生云只有一個感與應。所謂陰與陽。無處不是且如前後前便是陽後便是陰又如左右左便是陽右便是陰又如上下上面一截便是陽下面一截便是陰。又如問先生易說中謂伏羲作易驗陰陽消長兩端而已此語最盡曰陰陽雖是兩個字然却只是一氣之消息。一進一退一消一長進處便是陽退處便是陰長處便是陽。消處便是陰。只是這一氣之消長做出

tice, the middle Air is "the little snow," and the Light has already generated one part in thirty. A few days before the solstice twenty-seven or twenty-eight parts are already generated. On the day of the solstice then an entire stroke (—) is completed. It is not that yesterday it had no existence whatever, and to-day it returns complete in one morning. Speaking generally, when the Pŏh Diagram is completed, then this (Monad) is generated. Chang-tsze says that "formation and transmutation proceed imperceptibly; who can perceive them?" This is well said. As Lëĕ-tsze also, explaining their endless revolutions, says, that "Heaven and Earth alter imperceptibly; who can perceive their changes?" Every Air (*i. e.* soul) does not enter rapidly, nor does every bodily form fail suddenly, yet we can neither discern the formation nor the failing. Now the Light and Darkness decrease gradually and increase gradually; and Man's body from childhood to old age is precisely similar in this respect.

6. In the midst of Heaven and Earth there is only one Light and Darkness, and hence Mr. Ching says that there is only one influence and response. To exemplify what I said as to the Light and Darkness being omnipresent,— Before is Light, Behind is darkness; the Left side is Light, the Right side is Darkness; also, the upper portion of any thing is Light, and the lower part is Darkness. They asked the Teacher; The Yih-shwŏ (Commentary by Confucius) says that Fuh-he composed the Yih King with a view to the investigation of the decrease and increase of the two Principles Light and Darkness; is this statement complete? He replied, Although the Light and the Darkness are two designations, yet in reality they are but one Air which diminishes and accumulates,

古今天地間無限事來所以陰陽做一個說亦得做兩個說亦得。
又問氣之發散者爲陽。收歛者爲陰否曰也是如此如鼻氣之出入。
出者爲陽收回者爲陰入息如螺螄出殼了縮入相似是收入那出不盡底若只管出去不收便死矣問出入息畢竟出去時漸漸消到得出盡時便死否曰固是如此然那氣又只管生。
天地間一陰一陽。如環無端便是相勝底道理陰符經說天地之道浸故陰陽勝浸字最下得妙天地閒不陡頓恁地陰陽勝。
大抵言語兩端處皆有陰陽。如開物成務開物是陽。成務是陰。如致知力行致知是陽。力行是陰。周子之書屢發此意推之可見。
橫渠言遊氣紛擾合而成質者生人物之萬殊其陰陽兩端循環不已者。立天地之大義說得似稍支離只合云。陰陽五行。循環錯綜。

enters and recedes, decreases and increases. Entering it is Light, receding it is Darkness; increasing it is Light, and decreasing it is Darkness. It is this one Air decreasing and increasing, unlimitedly making every thing in the midst of Heaven and Earth, from ancient to modern times. Hence we can say that the Light and the Darkness are one (Air), and also that they are two (Airs).

7. Being further asked whether the Air producing and scattering is Light, and when contracting together is Darkness? He replied: That is also true; as for instance, the expiration and inspiration of the breath; expiration is Light, inspiration is Darkness. Inspiration resembles a snail which has come out of its shell, contracting into it again; it contracts and enters the inexhaustible foundation. If it merely came out without again contracting, then it would die. Being asked with regard to inspiration and expiration; when breathed forth, does the breath, in fact, gradually decrease until it is all entirely breathed forth, and then death takes place? He replied; It is just so: but that Air is being constantly generated (during life).

8. In the midst of Heaven and Earth the Light and Darkness alternate like a circle without beginning, mutually overcoming one another. The Yin Foo King says that the path of Heaven and Earth is gradual, and hence the Light and Darkness mutually overcome each other. This expression "gradual" is excellent. In the midst of Heaven and Earth there is no hurrying on, and thus the Light and the Darkness mutually overcome each other.

9. Every sentence, in its two parts, is Light and Darkness; for example, in the sentence "Opening out things and perfecting matters;" "Opening out things" is Light, and "perfecting matters" is Darkness. Also, in the sen-

升降往來所以生人物之萬殊立天地之大義。

問一故神曰橫渠說得極好須當子細看但近思錄所載與本書不同當時緣伯恭不肯全載故後來不曾與他添得一故神。橫渠親注云兩在故不測只是這一物却周行乎事物之間如所謂陰陽屈伸往來上下以至於行乎什百千萬之中無非這一個物事所以謂兩在故不測兩故化注云推行乎一凡天下之事一不能化。惟兩而後能化且如一陰一陽始能化生萬物雖是兩個要之亦是推行乎此一爾此說得極精須當與他子細看。神化兩字雖程子說得亦不甚分明惟是橫渠推出來推行有漸爲化合一不測爲神又曰一故神兩在故不測兩故化言兩在者或在陰或

tence "Perfecting Knowledge and diligently practising it;" "Perfecting Knowledge" is Light, and "diligently practising it" is Darkness. Chow-tsze's book conveys this idea in many passages, as may be seen on examination.

10. Hwăng-keu says, The abundant floating Air compresses and forms substance, generating the myriad distinctions in Men and things. It's two parts Light and Darkness revolve without ceasing, establishing the great goodness of Heaven and Earth.* There is a slight discrepancy here; he ought to have said, The Light and Darkness, and the Five Elements, revolve in a circle, intermixing, ascending and descending, going and coming; and thus, generating the myriad distinctions in Men and things, and establishing the great goodness of Heaven and Earth.

11. Being asked about the phrase "Unity, therefore God;" he replied: Hwăng-keu explains it excellently; his work ought to be carefully read. But, what the Kin Sze Lŭh states, does not accord with the original. Because at that time Pih-kung would not write it out completely, therefore no addition was afterwards made. "Unity, therefore God," Hwăng-keu, himself thus explains: He (God) is in both places (the Light and the Darkness), and is therefore Incomprehensible. It is just this one thing (God), which pervades the midst of matters and things; as for instance, the contracting and the expanding, the going and the coming, the ascending and the descending, of the Light and Darkness already mentioned. It thus pervades the midst of the myriad of things, so that nothing can be without this one thing. Hence it is said that He is in both places, and is therefore Incomprehensible. "Two, therefore He can transmute;" the Commentary explains that these emanate

---
* That is, every thing attaining its proper position, &c.

在陽。在陰時全體都是陰。在陽時全體都是陽。化是逐一挨將去底。一日復一日。一月復一月。節節挨將去便成一年。這是化。直卿云。一故神猶一動一靜互為其根兩故化猶動極而靜靜極復動。

橫渠言陰聚之陽必散之一段却見得陰陽之情。

五行一陰陽也陰陽一太極也太極本無極也。此當思無有陰陽而無太極底時節若以為止是陰陽却是形而下者若只專以理言則太極又不曾與陰陽相離正當沈潛玩索將圖象意思抽開細看又復合而觀之某解此云非有離乎陰陽也即陰陽而指其本體不雜乎陰陽而為言也。此句自有三節意思更宜深考通書云。靜而無動動而無靜物也。動而無動靜而無靜神也。當即此

from Unity. No one thing in the world can transmute of itself; there must always be *two* for that purpose, and then transmutation can take place. As for instance, when one Light and one Darkness exist, then these (being Male and Female) can generate the myriad of things. Although these are two, yet, in fact, they emanate forth from this Unity. These statements are most clear, and should be minutely examined into.

12. These two words "God" and "Transmutation," although Ching-tsze does not treat of them very clearly, yet Hwăng-keu has explained them. That which proceeds gradually is Transmutation; that which is united in one and is Incomprehensible is God. He also says, "Unity, therefore God; Two, therefore He can transmute," means that He is in both places; sometimes in the Darkness, and sometimes in the Light. When in the Darkness, His whole body is Darkness; and when He is in the Light, His whole body is Light. Transmutation is each thing succeeding in order. Day follows day; month follows month; each festival follows in rotation and completes each year; this is Transmutation. Chih-king says, that "Unity therefore God" resembles alternate Motion and Rest, the central point of which is their Root: "Two, therefore He can transmute," resembles moving to the utmost and resting, resting to the utmost and again moving.

13. Hwăng-keu says; The Darkness collects together, and the Light scatters. Thus he understands the natural disposition of the Light and the Darkness.

14. The Five Elements form one Light and Darkness; the Light and Darkness form one Great Extreme, and the Root of the Great Extreme is the Infinite.* This must

---

* 無 not, and 極 limit; the "ἄπειρον" of Western Philosophers.

兼看之。

問動而生陽靜而生陰注太極者本然之妙動靜者所乘之機太極只是理理不可以動靜言惟動而生陽靜而生陰理寓於氣不能無動靜所乘之機乘如乘載之乘其動靜者乃乘載在氣上不覺動了靜靜了又動曰然又問動靜無端陰陽無始那個動又從上面靜生下上面靜又是上面動生來今姑把這個說起曰然

問太極動而生陽是陽先動也今解云必體立而用得以行如何曰體自先有下言靜而生陰只是說相生無窮耳。

統言陰陽只是兩端而陰中自分陰陽陽中亦有陰陽乾道成男坤道成女男雖屬陽。而不可謂其無陰女雖屬陰。亦不可謂其無陽。

be regarded as the period when there was no Light and Darkness, and no Great Extreme. If we consider this Infinite to be merely the Light and Darkness (we are in error, for) these are assuredly corporeal; and if we consider it to be Fate, then the Great Extreme and the Light and Darkness had not yet become separated (so that it is different from either of these). You must diligently reflect upon this; take the diagrams, open them, and minutely investigate them; also place them together and examine them. I explain these statements thus: it (the Infinite) cannot be separated from the Light and Darkness; the Light and Darkness refer to its original body; and, we must not speak of it as being confounded with the Light and Darkness. These statements have these three meanings; you must examine them thoroughly. The Tung-shoo says: "That which when at Rest cannot Move, and when in Motion cannot Rest is Matter; that which Moves, yet moves not; Rests, yet rests not, is God." These statements should be compared.

15. Being asked as follows; "Moved and generated the Light, Rested and generated the Darkness" is explained to mean that the Great Extreme is the original self-existent Adorner; Motion and Rest are the spring upon which He rides. The Great Extreme is just Fate. We cannot predicate Motion and Rest of Fate alone; but, that which Moved and generated the Light, Rested and generated the Darkness, is Fate inherent in the Air, and which therefore cannot but Move and Rest. "The spring upon which He rides," that is, "rides" as in a chariot. His Motion and Rest are the result of his riding upon the Air, while He is not Himself affected by the perpetual Motion and Rest. Is this so? He replied, Just so. Being also asked; Motion and Rest have no beginning, the

人身氣屬陽。而氣有陰陽。血屬陰。而血有陰陽。

問陰陽動靜。以大體言則春夏是勤屬陽秋冬是靜屬陰。就一日言之晝陽而動夜陰而靜。就一時一刻言之無時而不動靜。無時而無陰陽日陰陽無處無之橫看豎看皆可見。橫看則左陽而右陰。豎看則上陽而下陰仰手則爲陽覆手則爲陰。向明處爲陽背明處爲陰。正蒙云陰陽之氣循環迭至聚散相盪升降相求絪縕相揉相兼相制欲一之不能蓋謂是也。

厚之問陽變陰合如何是合曰陽行而陰隨之。

陰陽有相對而言者如東陽西陰南陽北陰是也有錯綜而言者如晝夜寒暑一個橫一個直是也伊川言易變易也只説得相對底

Light and Darkness have no commencement; each Motion is generated from the previous Rest, and each Rest from the previous Motion; can we state the matter thus? He replied; yes.

16. The Great Extreme moved and generated the Light; does this mean that the Light moved first? The Commentators say that there must first be body, in order that the active part may act through it; how is this? He replied; body (*i. e. vis inertiæ*) must certainly exist first. The following sentence "Rested and generated the Darkness" just implies that they mutually generate each other without cessation.

17. Speaking generally, the Light and the Darkness are just two Principles, and the Darkness divides into Light and Darkness, as also the Light has Darkness as well as Light. Khëen perfects the Male, Khwăn the Female: although the Male belongs to the Light yet we cannot say that he is not Darkness, and although the Female belongs to the Darkness, we cannot say that she is not also Light. The Air of which Man's body is composed belongs to the Light, and yet it has both Light and Darkness; his blood *(anima)* belongs to the Darkness, and yet it has both Light and Darkness.

18. Being asked: When Light and Darkness, Motion and Rest are predicated of the whole body of the Universe; then, Spring and Summer are Motion and belong to the Light; Autumn and Winter are Rest and belong to the Darkness. With regard to a day, then the day-time is Light and Motion, and the night is Darkness and Rest. With regard to each hour and minute; not a single hour is without Motion and Rest or Light and Darkness. Is this so? He replied: There is no place whatever without the Light and Darkness. In the

陰陽流轉而已。不說錯綜底陰陽交互之理。言易須兼此二意。體在

天地後用起天地先對待底是體流行底是用體靜而用動〇以上語類二十條

陰陽只是一氣。陰氣流行卽爲陽。陽氣凝聚卽爲陰。非直有二物相

對也。此理甚明。周先生於太極圖中已言之矣。答楊元範

謂一陰一陽之謂道。已涉形器。五性爲形而下者恐皆未然。陰陽固

是形而下者。然所以一陰一陽者乃理也。形而上者也。五事固是

形而下者。然五常之性則理也。形而上者也。答楊子順

問蔡丈云。天根是好人之情狀月窟是小人之情狀。三十六宮是八

卦陰陽之爻。某疑人物二字恐未可便以善惡斷之。又言三十六

宮都是春卽月窟亦爲春也。曰陽善陰惡。聖賢如此說處極多。蓋

horizontal and perpendicular they can both be seen. In the horizontal the left is Light and the right is Darkness; in the perpendicular the upper part is Light and the lower part Darkness. The palm of the hand is Light, the back of the hand is Darkness. Opposite the light is Light, and the opposite side to the bright one is Darkness. The Ching Mung says that the Light and Dark Air revolve in a circle coming alternately, collecting and scattering, mutually agitating, ascending and descending, and mutually seeking each other; the male and female influences mutually entwining, mutually joining, and mutually ruling; they cannot be separated from each other. That is the explanation.

19. How-tsze asked: The Light changes, and the Darkness unites with it; what is this uniting? He replied: The Light moves on and the Darkness follows it.

20. The Light and Darkness may be regarded as opposites; as for instance, the East is Light and the West is Darkness; the South is Light, and the North is Darkness. They also may be regarded as intermingled; as for instance, day and night, cold and heat, horizontal and perpendicular. E-chuen says that "*yih*" signifies "Change;" this refers to the flowing forth and revolving Light and Darkness as opposites, and not to the intermingling Light and Darkness united in one. In speaking of Change we should unite both these ideas.

21. The Light and Darkness are merely one Air. The Dark Air flowing forth becomes Light, and the Light Air coagulating becomes Darkness: it is not that these are two mutually opposed things. This doctrine is very plain; Chow-tsze, in his diagram of the Great Extreme, explains it.

22. To say that the statement of the Yih King, that "The revolving Darkness—Light is Reason," refers to the

自正理而言。二者固不可相無以對待而言。則又各自有所主。康
節所詠恐是指生物之源而言則正氣爲人偏氣爲物。爲陰陽之
辨。季通所論却是推說然意亦通也。答甘
問蔡丈言天根爲好人之情狀月窟爲小人之情狀又云陰陽都將
做好說也得。以陰爲惡陽爲善亦得。伏蒙賜教以爲陽善陰惡。
賢如此說處極多蓋自正理而言。二者固不可相無以對待而言。
則又各有所主某疑康節先言天根月窟。是合偏正而言後言以
爲都是春者是專以正者言之不知是否曰看遺書中善惡皆天
理及惡亦不可不謂之性。不可以濁者不謂之水等語及易傳陽
無可盡之理一節卽此義可推矣。更以事實攷之只如鴟梟蝮蝎

Corporeal Receptacle;* or that the Five Natures (Benevolence, Rectitude, Propriety, Wisdom and Trustworthiness) are Corporeal, I fear is all incorrect. The Light and Darkness are Corporeal, but that which makes them to be the alternating Light and Darkness is Fate which is Incorporeal. The Five Matters are Corporeal, but the Nature of these Five Constant Virtues is Fate, which is Incorporeal.

23. One asked about the statement of Tsae-chang, that Heaven's Root is the good man's disposition, and the Moon's cavern is the mean man's disposition. The thirty-six Palaces are merely the strokes of the Light and Darkness of the Eight Diagrams. I suppose that we cannot decidedly predicate Good and Evil of both Men and things? Moreover, he says that the thirty-six Palaces are all Spring; the Moon's cavity therefore must also be Spring? (*i. e.* because the thirty-six include both the Light and Darkness). He replied: the Light is Good, and the Darkness is Evil; both Sages and Worthies have frequently made this statement. Now speaking strictly, of these two, neither can be non-existent (in anything). Speaking of them as opposites, then each is independent of the other. What Kang-tsëĕ states refers, I suppose, to the Origin of every living thing, so that the upright Air is Man, and the depraved Air is things; and this is the difference between the Light and the Darkness. What Ke-tung states is an enlargement on the subject, but the meaning is also correct.

24. One asked: Tsae-chang says, "Heaven's Root is the natural disposition of the good man, and the Moon's cavern is the natural disposition of the mean man." He also says we can assert that both the Light and Darkness are Good, as well as that the Darkness is Evil and the

---

* That is, the twofold Air (氣) in which Reason is inherent.

惡草毒藥。還可道不是天地陰陽之氣所生否。管吉甫

天地之間所以為造化者陰陽二氣之終始盛衰而已。陽生於北。長於東而盛於南陰始於南中於西而終於北。故陽常居左而以生育長養為功。其類則為剛為明。為公為義。而凡君子之道屬焉。陰常居右而以夷傷慘殺為事其類則為柔為暗。為私為利而凡小人之道屬焉。聖人作易畫卦繫辭於其進退消長之際。所以示人者深矣。傅伯撝字序

陰陽之氣相勝而不能相無。其為善惡之象則異乎此蓋以氣言則動靜無端。陰陽無始其本固並立而無先後之序善惡之分也若以善惡之象而言則人之性本獨有善而無惡其為學亦欲去惡

Light is Good. We have your instruction to the effect that the Light is Good and the Darkness is Evil, and that the Sages and Worthies frequently state this; that, speaking with reference to correct principles, neither of these can be non-existent (in anything); and speaking of them as opposites, then each is independent of the other. I suppose that Kang-tsëĕ's first statement about Heaven's Root and the Moon's cavity refers to the depraved and upright (Air) united together as one; and that what he afterwards says about *both* being Spring (*i. e.* Good) only refers to the upright portion (of the twofold Air); is this so? He replied: Looking over the works handed down to us, Good and Evil are both Heavenly Principles, and we cannot assert that Evil is not also Nature (as well as Good); just as we cannot say that the sediment does not partake of the nature of water. Also the Yih Chuen says that "The Light alone cannot complete Fate;" (*i. e.* the Light and Darkness *both* form the ethereal body of Fate); we can understand the meaning from this statement. Moreover, we can take existing things and examine this matter; as for instance, the *Che-këaou*,* serpents, scorpions, weeds, and poisons;—can we venture to affirm that these are not generated by the Light-Dark Air of Heaven and Earth?

25. That which fills up the midst of Heaven and Earth, so that these can make and transmute, is the twofold Air Light and Darkness which cause termination and commencement, increase and decline. The Light is generated at the North, spreads out to the East, and fills up (the semicircle) to the South. The Darkness commences at the South, fills up (the circle) to the West, and terminates at the North. Hence the Light always dwells upon the left

---

* A bird that is said to eat its parent.

而全善。不復得以不能相無者而爲言矣。今以陰陽爲善惡之象。
而又曰不能相無。故必曰小人曰爲不善。而善心未嘗不間見以
爲陰不能無陽之證。然則曷不曰君子曰爲善。而惡心亦未嘗不
間見以爲陽不能無陰之證耶。蓋亦知其無是理矣。且又曰克盡
己私。純是義理。亦不離乎陰陽之正。則善固可以無惡矣。所謂不
能相無者。又安在耶。大凡義理精微之際。合散交錯。其變無窮。而
不相違悖且以陰陽善惡論之。則陰陽之正皆善也其沴皆惡。而
以象類言。則陽善而陰惡。以動靜言則陽客而陰主。

周子所謂剛善剛惡
柔亦如之者是也

此類甚多。要當大其心以觀之。不可以一說拘也。 答王子合

陰陽盈天地之間。其消息闔闢。終始萬物。觸目之間。有形無形。無非

(the East), and to generate, nourish, cause to grow, and to cherish, is its province. Its species are the hard, the bright, the impartial and the upright, and the path of every Model Man belongs to it. The Darkness always dwells on the right (the West), and to hurt, wound, injure, and destroy, is its occupation. Its species are the soft, the dark, the selfish, and the covetous, and the path of every mean man belongs to it. The Sage invented the Diagrams of the Yih King in order to explain these, with their entering and receding, decreasing and increasing; hence the instruction they afford is deep.

26. The Light and Dark Air mutually conquer and neither of them can be regarded as non-existent. Regarding them as the *simulacra* of Good and Evil, the case is different. For, with regard to the Air, then, Motion and Rest have no beginning, the Light and Darkness have no commencement. As to origin they pair together, and there is no distinction of priority or posteriority, Good or Evil, between them. If we speak in reference to the *simulacra* of Good and Evil, then Man's Nature is intrinsically Good, and has no Evil in it. When educated he still desires to cast away Evil and to complete Goodness, and we cannot speak of him as not being exclusively the one (*i. e.* Good to the exclusion of Evil). Now, if we speak of the Light and Darkness as the *simulacra* of Good and Evil and also say that neither of these can be non-existent, then we must allow that while the mean man does Evil daily, yet his Good heart is not, at times, unmanifested, showing clearly that the Darkness cannot exist without the Light. But then, why can we not say, that the Model Man is daily Good, and yet his Evil heart, is not, at times, unmanifested, in order to prove that the Light cannot exist without the Darkness? Thus we see

是也。而蘇氏以爲象立而陰陽隱凡可見者皆物也。非陰陽也失其理矣。達陰陽之本者固不指生物而謂之陰陽。亦不別求陰陽於物象見聞之外也。

蘇氏易解辨

一陰一陽往來不息舉道之全體而言莫著於此者矣。而以爲借陰陽以喻道之似。則是道與陰陽各爲一物借此而況彼也。陰陽之端。動靜之機而已動極而靜靜極而動故陰中有陽陽中有陰未有獨立而孤居者此一陰一陽所以爲道也今日一陰一陽者。陰陽未交而物未生廓然無一物不可謂之無有者道之似也。然則道果何物乎。此皆不知道之所以爲道而欲以虛無寂滅之學揣摸而言之故其說如此。

蘇氏易解辨

夫謂溫厚之氣盛於東南嚴凝之氣盛於西北者禮家之說也謂陽

(from the absurdity of the latter proposition) that there is no such doctrine. Moreover, if we assert that by completely overcoming our own depravity, and becoming thoroughly Good, we never separate from the upright portion of the Light and Darkness, then, Good can exist without Evil, and what becomes of what has been already said as to the one not existing without the other? Speaking generally, the limits of the pure and minute Goodness unite and scatter and mingle together; their changes are endless, and they do not oppose each other. Moreover, with regard to the Light and Darkness, Good and Evil, the upright portion of the Light and Darkness is wholly Good, and their noxious portion is wholly Evil. With regard to the species of these *simulacra*, then the Light is Good and the Darkness is Evil; with regard to Motion and Rest, then the Light is guest, and the Darkness is host; these species are numerous. All this should be carefully looked into, and not determined by a *single* statement.

27. The Light and Darkness fill up the midst of Heaven and Earth; they decrease and increase, shut and open, terminate and commence the myriad of things; and of every thing which strikes the eye, whether corporeal or incorporeal, not a single thing is without them. Shooshe considers that their *simulacra* are substantial while the Light and Darkness themselves are hidden; that, every thing which is visible is material, and is not Light and Darkness. This doctrine is incorrect. To understand the root of the Light and the Darkness we must not point to existing things and call *them* Light and Darkness; and also, we must not seek these in some other place *outside* those things which are visible.

28. The alternating Light and Darkness, coming and

生於子。於卦爲復。陰生於午。於卦爲姤者。曆家之說也。謂巽位東南。乾位西北者。說卦之說也。此三家者各爲一說。而禮家曆家之言猶可相通至於說卦則其卦位自爲一說。而與彼二者不相謀矣。今來敎乃欲合而一之。而其間又有一說之中自相乖戾者。此某所以不能無疑也。夫謂東南以一陰已生而爲陰柔之位。西北以一陽已生。而爲陽剛之位。則是陽之盛於春夏者不得爲陽。陰之盛於秋冬者不得爲陰。而反以其始生之微者爲主也。謂一陰生於東南一陽生於西北則是陰不生於正南午位之遘。而淫於東陽不生於正北子位之復。而旅於西也。謂巽以一陰之生而位乎東南則乾者豈一陽之生。而位於西北乎。況說卦之本文於巽則但取其潔齊於乾則㊣取其戰而已。而未嘗有一陰一陽始生

going without cessation is the complete bodily substance of Reason. Nothing can be plainer than this; but, to imagine that we can take the Light and Darkness and institute a comparison between them and Reason, this is to suppose Reason and the Light and Darkness to be each separate from the other, and to take the one and add it to the other. The commencement of the Light and Darkness is nothing more than the spring of Motion and Rest; moving to the utmost and resting, resting to the utmost and moving. Hence in the Darkness is Light, and in the Light there is Darkness; neither existing separately from the other. It is in this way that the alternating Light and Darkness are said to be Reason.* They say now, in reference to the alternating Light and Darkness, that before this Light and Darkness had intercourse with each other and things were generated, when not a single thing existed, that then Reason cannot be said to have been non-existent. But, according to this, what is Reason? All this is ignorance of the way in which Reason comes to be Reason, and resembles the mystical school. It is merely guessing; and hence they speak thus.

29. With regard to the warm and genial Air accumulating at the south-east, and the harsh, coagulated Air accumulating on the north-west; these are the statements of the Ritualists. That the Light is generated in the *Tsze* (*Hwuy*) in the *Fŭh* Diagram; the Darkness in the *Woo* (*Hwuy*) in the *Kow* Diagram; are the statements of the Astronomers. That the throne of the *Seuen* Diagram is the south-east, and that the throne of *Khëen* is the north-west, are the statements of the Diviners. These three schools each express themselves differently;

---

* That is, the Light and Dark Air emanates from the Divine Reason, and the latter is inherent in it; these are *distinct* but not *separate things*.

之說也。凡此崎嶇反復終不可通。不若直以陽剛爲仁。陰柔爲義
之明白而簡易也。蓋如此。則發生爲仁。肅殺爲義。三家之說皆無
所悟。肅殺雖似乎剛。然實天地收斂退藏之氣。自不妨其爲陰柔
也。

答袁機仲

論十二卦。則陽始於子。而終於巳。陰始於午。而終於亥。論四時之氣
則陽始於寅。而終於未。陰始於申。而終於丑。此一說者雖若小差。
而所爭不過二位。蓋子位一陽雖生而未出乎地。至寅位泰卦則
三陽之生方出地上。而溫厚之氣從此始焉。巳位乾卦六陽雖極。
而溫厚之氣未終。故午位一陰雖生。而未害於陽。必至未位遯卦
而後溫厚之氣始盡也。其午位陰已生。而嚴凝之氣及申方始亥
位六陰雖極。而嚴凝之氣。至丑方盡。義亦倣此。蓋地中之氣難見。

and the statements of the Ritualists and Astronomers may possibly be reconciled. With regard to the Diviners, the position of the Diagrams depends upon their own statements alone, and they differ from both the other schools. In the present communication these three are treated as one, and yet statements are made which are inconsistent with such an idea, and which make it positively doubtful. Now, to assert that at the south-east point a Darkness is already generated, and that this point is the throne of the Darkness and softness; that, at the north-west a Light is already generated, and that this point is the throne of the Light and Darkness; then, the accumulated Light in Spring and Summer cannot be regarded as Light, and the accumulated Darkness in Autumn and Winter, cannot be regarded as Darkness. This is, on the contrary, to regard what is only their minute commencement, as their full power. If we assert that a complete Darkness is generated at the south-east and a complete Light at the north-west; then, the Darkness is not generated at the exact south at the *Woo* throne, but erroneously goes to the east; and the Light is not generated at the exact north, at *Tsze*, the throne of the *Fŭh* Diagram, but lingers at the west. To say that the *Seuen* Diagram is generated by a Darkness, and has its throne upon the south-east, then, is not this to consider that *Khëen* is generated by a Light and that its throne is upon the north-west? Moreover, with regard to the original Diagrams, these allude only to their purity and completness in the *Seuen*, and to their contending in the *Khëen*, and nothing more; and do not assert any thing about the commencement of the generation of each Light and Darkness. All this, therefore, is irregular, and in fact, perfectly unintelligible. It is not so clear or laconic as just to consider the Light

而地上之氣易識。故周人以建子為正雖得天統而孔子之論為邦乃以夏時為正蓋取其陰陽始終之著明也。按圖以推其說可見。

答袁機仲

來諭以東南之溫厚為仁西北之嚴凝為義此鄉飲酒義之言也然本其言雖分仁義而無陰陽柔剛之別但於其後復有陽氣發於東方之說則固以仁為屬乎陽。而義之當屬乎陰。從可推矣。來諭乃不察此而必欲以仁為剛。以義為柔。於是強以溫厚為柔嚴凝為剛。不可屬乎陽。剛之不可屬乎陰也。又移北之陰以就南而使主乎仁之柔移南之陽以就北而使主乎義之剛。其於方位氣候悉反易之。而其所以為說者率皆參差乖迕而不可合又使東北之為陽西南之為陰亦皆得其半而失

and Hard to be Benevolence, and the Darkness and Soft to be Rectitude; for thus, to generate will be Benevolence, and to destroy will be Rectitude; and then the statements of the three schools are all reconciled. Although destruction resembles the Hard, yet, in reality, the collected and stored up Air of Heaven and Earth may, without objection, be considered Darkness and Soft.

30. With regard to the 12 Diagrams,* the Light commences at *Tsze* and ends at *Sze*; the Darkness commences at *Woo*, and ends at *Hae*. With regard to the Air of the four seasons, then the Light commences at *Yin*, and ends at *Wei*; the Darkness commences at *Shin*, and ends at *Chaou*. Although these divisions (of the circle) are slightly different, yet the difference only extends to two thrones (one commencing at *Tsze* and the other at *Yin*). In the *Tsze* throne, although one (part) Light is generated and does not come forth from the (formed) Earth, yet, arrived at the *Yin* throne, the *T'ae* Diagram, then, three Lights are generated and come forth above the Earth, and the warm genial Air commences from this point. At the *Sze* throne, the *Khëen* Diagram, although the extreme limit of six Lights, yet the warm, genial Air has not ended; and therefore, at the *Woo* throne, although one Darkness is generated, and does not injure the Light, yet, arrived at the *Wei* throne, the *Tun* Diagram, the Air which succeeds the warm and genial Air, begins to draw to a close. At the *Woo* throne the Darkness is already generated, and the coagulated Air commences at *Shin*. At the *Hae* throne, although the extreme limit of six Darknesses, yet the coagulated Air is exhausted at the *Chaou* throne. Rectitude also resembles this. Now the Air in the midst of the Earth is diffi-

---

* See Plate, Part III, par. 5 & 6. Notes.

其半。愚於圖子已具見其失矣。蓋嘗論之。陽主進而陰主退。陽主息而陰主消。進而息者其氣強。退而消者其氣弱。此陰陽之所以爲柔剛也。陽剛溫厚居東南主春夏。而以作長爲事。陰柔嚴凝居西北主秋冬。而以斂藏爲事。作長爲生。斂藏爲殺。此剛柔之所以爲仁義也。以此觀之。則陰陽剛柔仁義之位。豈不曉然。而彼揚子雲之所謂於仁也柔。於義也剛者。乃自其用處之末流言之所謂於仁也柔。於義也剛者。乃自其用處之末流言之。蓋亦所謂陽中之陰。陰中之陽。固不妨自爲一義。但以雜乎此而不論之爾。

答袁機仲〇以上文集十一條

cult to discern, but the Air above the Earth is easy to be recognised; therefore the people of the Chow Dynasty established *Tsze* to be the first throne. Although they thus obtained the Complete Heaven* yet, according to the instructions of Confucius concerning government, they took the Hea Dynasty time to be the first throne (*i.e. Yin*); thus making plain the commencement and termination of the Light and Darkness. On examining the diagram this explanation will be clear.

31. The present communication considers the warm and genial Air of the south-east to be Benevolence, and the coagulated Air of the north-west to be Rectitude. This is the statement of the *Hëang-yin-tsëw-e*. But, if we take this as our authority, although it distinguishes Benevolence and Rectitude, yet it does not discriminate between the Light and Darkness, the Soft and the Hard. But, afterwards, there is another statement to the effect that the Light Air issues forth on the east; thus taking Benevolence to belong to the Light, and Rectitude to belong to the Darkness, as may be deduced from this. The present communication shows want of examination into this, and considers Benevolence to be Soft, and Rectitude to be Hard; this is a mistake. A further mistake is that the Soft cannot belong to the Light, nor the Hard to the Darkness; and thus, the warm and genial Air is forced to be Soft, and the coagulated to be Hard. Moreover it removes the northern Darkness to the south, causing it to rule over the Softness of Benevolence; and removes the southern Light to the north, causing it to rule over the Hardness of Rectitude. This is to reverse the position of the thrones, and the origin of such statements

---

* Heaven emerges from Chaos in the 子 period, during the twilight of the world, when $\frac{1}{10}$ portion of the Light is generated.

問前日先生答書云。陰陽五行之爲性。各是一氣所禀。而性則一也。
兩性字同否。曰。一般又曰。同者理也。不同者氣也。又曰。他所以道
五行之生各一其性節復問這個莫是木自是木火自是火。而其
理則一先生應而曰。且如這個光也。有在硯蓋上底。也有在墨上
底。其光則一也。以下論五行
氣之精英者爲神。金木水火土非神。所以爲金木水火土者是神。在
人則爲理。所以爲仁義禮智信者是也。
金木水火土雖曰五行各一其性。然一物又各具五行之理不可不
知康節却細推出來。
天一自是生水。地二自是生火。生水只是合下便具得濕底意思。木

is utter confusion and perverseness: they cannot be reconciled together. Moreover, to make the north-east the Light, and the south-west the Darkness, is partly correct and partly incorrect. I have already traced all these errors on the diagram. Now, to explain the matter; the Light rules over entering, and the Darkness over receding; the Light rules over increase and the Darkness over decrease. Entering and increasing, the Air is strong; receding and decreasing, the Air is weak: it is thus that the Light and Darkness are Hard and Soft. The Light is Hard, warm and genial, dwells at the south-east, and rules over the Spring and Summer; and to cause growth is its province. The Darkness is Soft and congealed, dwells on the north-west, rules over the Autumn and Winter, and to gather in and store up is its province. Growth is Life; gathering in and storing up is Death; and it is thus that the Hard and the Soft are Benevolence and Rectitude. Thus examining the matter, are not the thrones of the Light and the Darkness, the Hard and the Soft, Benevolence and Rectitude, apparent? And, as **to** the statement of *Yang Tsze-yun*, that Benevolence is also Soft, and Rectitude also Hard, this refers to their activity not flowing forth. Now, as to what has been said about Darkness being in the Light, and Light in the Darkness; his meaning does not differ from this: but we must not confound this with the other statements in our explanations.

32. Being asked; You sir, formerly answered a letter to the effect that the Light and Darkness, and the Five Elements, constitute Nature; that each is conferred by the one Air (The Great Monad) and that Nature is Monad. Has the term "Nature" the same meaning in these statements? He replied; it has. He said moreover; That

便是生得一個軟底金便是生出得一個硬底五行之說正蒙中
說得好又曰木者土之精華也又曰水火不出於土正蒙一段說
得最好不胡亂下一字
問黃寺丞云金木水火體質屬土曰正蒙有一說好只說金與木之
體質屬土水與火却不屬土問火附木而生莫亦屬土否曰火自
是個虛空中物事問只溫熱之氣便是火否曰然
水火清金木濁土又濁
論陰陽五行曰康節說得法密橫渠說得理透邵伯溫載伊川言曰
向惟見周茂叔語及此然不及先生之有條理也欽夫以爲伊川
未必有此語蓋伯溫妄載某則以爲此語恐誠有之

which is unchangeable is Fate, and that which is diverse is the Air (Monad). He also remarked that it (the letter) therefore states, with regard to the generation of the Five Elements, that each has its own Nature. It is now further inquired whether this does not mean, that Wood is spontaneously Wood, and Fire is spontaneously Fire, and their (inherent) Fate is Unity.* The teacher replied, it is just like the Light upon the cover of this inkstone, and also upon the ink; that Light is but one.

33. The pure and bright portion of the Air is God; Metal, Wood, Water, and Earth are not God; but he who makes them to be Metal, Wood, Water, Fire, and Earth, is God. In Man this is Fate, which causes him to possess Benevolence, Rectitude, Propriety, Wisdom, and Trustworthiness.

34. Although Metal, Wood, Water, Fire and Earth, are called the Five Elements, each having its own Nature; yet, each has the Fate of the Five Elements (*i.e.* as one Air) inherent in it. We should not be ignorant of this. Kang-tsëĕ has already explained it minutely.

35. Heaven is Monad and spontaneously generated Water; the Earth is Duad, and spontaneously generated Fire. Generating Water merely means that when these united together the whole mass was moist. Wood is merely the generation of a Soft; Metal, the generation of a Hard. The explanation given of the Five Elements in the *Ching-mung* is correct: it says, that Wood is the subtile and clear portion of Earth; and also, that Fire and Water do not come out of Earth. These statements of the *Ching-mung* are very correct, and not one word is redundant.

---

* That is, the *indivisible* one; Monad is the *divisible* one. The number "*one*" therefore, in Cosmogony, is Unity inherent in Monad. This was also the "one" of Pythagoras.

陰以陽為質。陽以陰為質。水內明而外暗。火內暗而外明。橫渠曰。陰陽之精互藏其宅正此意也。

清明內影。濁明外影。清明金水。濁明火日。

陽變陰合初生水火。水火氣也。流動閃鑠。其體尚虛。其成形猶未定。

次生木金。則確然有定形矣。水火初是自生木金則資於土五金之屬皆從土中旋生出來。

大抵天地生物先其輕清以及重濁天一生水。地二生火。二物在五行中最輕清。金木復重於水火。土又重於金木。如論律呂則又重濁為先宮最重濁。商次之角次之徵又次之羽最後。<small>以上語類十一條</small>

陰陽之為五行。有分而言之者。如木火陽而金水陰也。有合而言之

36. Being asked: Hwang She-ching says, the material substance of Metal, Wood, Water, and Fire, belong to Earth; is this so? He replied: The *Ching-mung* says well, that only the material substance of Metal and Wood belong to Earth; Water and Fire do not belong to Earth. Being asked: Fire depends upon Wood for generation, does it not therefore belong to Earth? He replied: Fire is a thing in the midst of the vast Vacuum. Being asked whether it is merely the hot Air which is Fire? He replied; yes.

37. Water and Fire are the subtile (Air); Metal and Wood are the gross (Air); and Earth is still grosser (Air).

38. Discoursing about the Light and Darkness and the Five Elements, he said that Kang-tsëe's explanation is profound; Hwang-keu's is clear; Shaou Pih-wăn records the explanation of E-chuen saying, "I formerly only saw Chow Mow-shŭh's explanation, but it does not equal the precepts of my Master." Khin-foo considers that E-chuen ought not to have expressed himself so, and supposes that Pih-wăn charges him falsely. But I think that the statement was really made.

39. The Light is the *substans* of the Darkness; and the Darkness is the *substans* of the Light. Water is bright within and Dark without; Fire is dark within and bright without. Hwang-keu says, the subtile portions of the Light and Darkness are concealed in their central point; the meaning is the same.

40. Subtile brightness has the shadow within; dull brightness throws it without. Metal and Water have subtile brightness; Fire and the Sun have dull brightness.

41. The Light changes and the Darkness responds, at first generating Water and Fire. This Water and Fire are the Air, flowing forth and flashing brightly; their bodily substance is immaterial, and the forms which

者。如木之甲火之丙土之戊金之庚水之壬皆陽。而乙丁己辛癸皆陰也。以此推之健順五常之理可見。

答黃商伯

問一曰水二曰火三曰木四曰金五曰土竊謂氣之初溫而已溫則蒸溽蒸溽則條達條達則堅凝堅凝則有形質五者雖一有俱有。然推其先後之序理或如此日向見吳斗南說五事庶徵皆當依此爲序其言亦有理。

答黃商伯

問二氣五行造化萬物一闔一闢萬變是生所謂五行之氣卽雷風水火之運耶又卽二氣之叄差散殊者耶先儒謂物物皆具則人之氣禀有偏重者謂之皆具可乎。或謂雖物皆具而就五行之中。有得其多者有得其少者於此思之殊茫然未曉曰五行之氣。如

they should assume were undetermined. Secondly, they generated Wood and Metal; and then their forms were determined. Water and Fire were spontaneously generated at first, Wood and Metal then commenced from Earth. The five kinds of metals were successively produced from Earth.

42. Speaking generally Heaven and Earth generated things, their light and pure (Air) being first, and then their heavy and gross. Heaven is Monad (Shang-te) and generated Water, the Earth is Duad and generated Fire; and these two things are the most subtile and pure portions of the Five Elements. Metal and Wood are heavier than Water and Fire; Earth is also heavier than Metal or Wood. To illustrate this by the notes in music; the heavier and coarser notes are first. *Kung* is the most heavy and coarse note, *Shang* is next, *Këŏ* is next to that, then comes *Ch'ing*, and *Yu* is last.

43. Dividing and treating of the Light and Darkness considered as the Five Elements, then Wood and Fire are the Light, and Metal and Water are the Darkness. Speaking of them unitedly (*i. e.* as one Air), then the *Këa* of Wood, the *Ping* of Fire, the *Mow* of Earth, the *Kăng* of Metal, and the *Jin* of Water are all Light; and *Yih, Ting, Sze, Sin,* and *Kwei*, are all Darkness. Examining into this, you can understand the doctrine of the strength or yielding of the Five constant (virtues).

44. Being asked: The first (Element) is called Water, the second Fire, the third Wood, the fourth Metal, and the fifth Earth. I suppose this arrangement means that the Air at the beginning was warm, and being warm it then ascended as hot vapour. This ascending vapour then spread out (like a bud); spreading out it coagulated, and when coagulated it had substantial form. Although these Five (elements) all existed at the same moment, yet,

溫涼寒暑燥濕剛柔之類盈天地之間者皆是。舉一物無不具此五者。但其間有多少分數耳。五音五色五味之類皆是也。○答呂子約

問以質而語其生之序。則曰水火木金土。而水木陽也。火金陰也。此豈就圖而指其序耶。而水木何以謂之陽。火金何以謂之陰。曰天一生水。地二生火。天三生木。地四生金。一三陽也。二四陰也。答林子玉

問以氣而語其行之序。則木火土金水。而木火何以謂之陽。金水何以謂之陰。曰此以四時而言。春夏爲陽。秋冬爲陰。此豈卽其運用處而言之耶。答林子玉○以土文集五條

問學者云。古人排十二時是如何。諸生思未得。先生云志

examining into their order of priority and posteriority, it is, I suppose, as has been stated? He replied: I formerly saw a statement by Woo Tsow-nan, that the Five senses,* and the General Regulators,† ought all to be thus arranged; this statement is correct.

45. Being asked with regard to the two Airs and the Five Elements, making and transmuting the myriad of things. At the alternate shuttings and openings (of the Universe), the myriad of changes are generated. That which is called the Air of the Five Elements is the revolving Thunder, Wind, Water and Fire, and also the mingling and scattering of the two Airs. Former scholars say that these are inherent in each thing: but, the Air which Man receives has deflections; can it then be said to pervade all things? Some say that although all things possess these (*i.e.* both the Good and Evil Air) yet, in the midst of the Five Elements they are received in different proportions. These statements are confused and unintelligible? He replied: The species of the Air of the Five Elements, for exanple, Warm, Cool, Heat, Cold, Dry, Moist, Hard, and Soft, all fill up the midst of Heaven and Earth. Take any one thing, and it contains these Five Elements; but some things obtain them in a greater, some in a lesser proportion.

46. Being asked: Speaking of the order of their generation with regard to their substance, then it is said of Water, Fire, Wood, Metal, and Earth, that Water and Wood are Light, and Fire and Metal are Darkness. Does this refer to their order in the Diagram? And then, how can Water and Wood be designated Light, and Fire and Metal Darkness? He replied: Heaven is Monad (Shangte) and generated Water; the Earth is Duad and gene-

---

* Shape, Speech, Sight, Hearing and Thinking.
† Rain, Fair weather, Heat, Cold and Wind.

字從之從心乃是心之所之古時字從之從日亦是日之所至蓋日至於午則謂之午時至未則謂之未時十二時皆如此推古者訓日字實也月字缺也月則有缺時日常實是如此如天行亦有差月星行又遲趕他不上惟日鐵定如此又云看北斗可以見天之行 以下論時令

只是算氣之節候大率只是一個氣陰陽播而為五行

五行中各有陰陽甲乙木丙丁火春屬木夏屬火年月日時無有非五行之氣甲乙丙丁又屬陰屬陽只是二五之氣人之生適遇其氣有得清者有得濁者貴賤壽夭皆然故有參錯不齊如此

rated Fire; Heaven, the Triad, generated Wood; the Earth, Tetrad, generated Metal. The Monad and Triad are Light, the Dyad and Tetrad are Darkness.

47. Being asked: Speaking of the order of their motion, with regard to their Air; then, they are Wood, Fire, Earth, Metal, and Water; and, Wood and Fire are Light, Metal and Water are Darkness; is not this speaking of them with regard to their revolutions? Yet, how can Wood and Fire be called Light, and Metal and Water Darkness? He replied: This refers to the Four Seasons; the Spring and Summer are Light, Autumn and Winter are Darkness.

48. He asked his pupils how the ancients arranged the twelve hours? They could not explain this. The teacher said: The character *Che* is formed of *Che* and *Sin*, and it means what the mind does (*i. e.* reflects). The ancient character *She*, was formed from *Che* and *Jih*, and is what days limit. For, when the day arrives at *Woo*, it is called the *Woo* time; and when it arrives at *Wei*, it is called the *Wei* time; all the twelve hours are to be explained thus. The ancients explain the character *Jih* (Sun) as "solid," and *Yuĕ* (Moon) as "broken off;" the Moon at times being deficient, but the Sun being always full. The case is so. Thus Heaven's revolutions have also irregularity; the Moon and Stars also, are slow and cannot overtake it; but the Sun is, as it were, fixed like iron. He further said; Look at Ursa Major, and then you can perceive the revolutions of Heaven.

49. Number is merely the calculation of the times and seasons of the Air. Speaking generally this is merely one Air; the Light and Darkness scatter and become the Five Elements, and each of these Five Elements has the Light and Darkness inherent in it. *Këa-yih* is Wood, *Ping-ting* is Fire: Spring belongs to Wood, and Summer

陽變陰合。而生水火木金土陰陽氣也。生此五行之質。天地生物。五行獨先地卽是土土便包含許多金木之類天地之間何事而非五行。五行陰陽。七者滾合便是生物底材料。五行順布四時行焉。金木水火分屬春夏秋冬。土則寄旺四季。如春屬木而清明後十二日卽是土寄旺之時。每季寄旺十八日。共七十二日唯夏季十八日。土氣爲最旺。故能生秋金也。以圖象考之。木生火金生水之類各有小畫相牽連。而火生土土生金。獨穿乎土之內。餘則從旁而過。爲可見矣。<small>以上言類三條</small>

to Fire. As to Years, Months, Days and Hours, not one of these is devoid of the Air of the Five Elements. *Këa-yih* and *Ping-ting* belong both to the Light and the Darkness; that is to the Air of the Two and the Five.* Men at their birth obtain this Air, some the pure portion, and some the coarse; the honourable and the mean, the old and the young, are all thus. Hence irregularity and difference arise.

50. The Light changes and the Darkness pairs with it, and they generate Water, Fire, Wood, Metal and Earth. The Light-Dark Air generates the substance of these Five Elements. When Heaven and Earth generate things, the Five Elements alone are first obtained. The Earth is just earth, which enfolds every description of metal and wood. In the midst of Heaven and Earth, what single thing has not the Five Elements? The Five Elements, the Light and the Darkness, are seven things revolving together, and are just the materials from which things are generated. The Five Elements submissively spread out, and the Four Seasons revolve. Metal, wood, water and fire severally belong to Spring, Summer, Autumn and Winter, and earth is inherent in and adorns each of the Four Seasons. For example, Spring belongs to wood, and twelve days after the feast of *Tsing-ming* is the time when earth rests in, and adorns it. Each Season has eighteen days thus rested in and adorned (by earth); seventy-two days in all. Only, during the eighteen days of the Summer Season, the earth Air is most brilliant, and hence it can generate the Autumn metal.

---

* That is Heaven and Earth and the Five Elements.

Take the diagram and examine this. Wood generates fire, and metal generates water; each has a small stroke which connects them together in their revolutions. Fire generates earth, and earth generates metal, so that each penetrates to the interior of earth. There are other lines which pass along from the sides and show this.*

---

* See Plate III, Chinese arrangement, for these small lines connecting the Five Elements.

NOTES.

FATE AND AIR.

(PARAGRAPH, I.) In this "General Treatise," Choo-tsze commences by stating the theory of the Confucianists as to the component parts of the Great Origin of all things. These two parts are, an Immaterial Principle which he designates "Fate," and a Material Principle, viz., "Air," the Infinite, Eternal, Primordial Matter, in which the former is always inherent, and from, as well as by which every portion of the Kosmos is formed.

The Confucianists agree with all other pagan Philosophers in their fundamental tenet that "*ex nihilo nihil fit*," and they therefore hold, in common with the latter, the eternity of Matter. As to what the Primordial Matter is, Western Philosophers differed amongst themselves; some supposing it to be Water, as Thales did; some, Fire, as Heraclitus and Zeno. The Confucianists, however, like the philosopher Anaximenes and others, consider it to be an Infinite, Eternal Air. Heaven is made from this Air, so is Earth, so are Gods and Demons, so is Man, and so also are Birds, Beasts, Reptiles, Insects, Trees, Plants, Mountains, Rivers, &c. And, as each of these several parts of the Universe, (which is one whole and yet all things), is made from Air, so also each has got the Eternal "Fate" inherent in it; for, there is no such thing in the whole Universe as Air without Fate inherent in it, or as Fate existing by itself, separate from the Primordial Air. The Great Origin of all things, therefore, is an Eternal Fate inherent in an Infinite, Eternal mass of Air, or Primordial Matter.

What this "Fate" is, Choo-tsze himself informs us elsewhere, *e. gr.* "Fate" is God (神), and is Incomprehensible." "Being asked whether the God (神) spoken of is the Maker and Transmuter of Heaven and Earth, he (Choo-tsze) replied, God (神) is just that Fate." "God (神) is the Lord of Change (*i. e.* the ever-changing Primordial Air) and hence He is Omnipresent."[1] "Separated from Air there is no God (神); and separated from God (神) there is no Air."[2] "All things have visible traces, but God (神) who is in their midst is invisible. God (神) is never separate from Matter. Hence God (神) is the Incomprehensible Being who is in the midst of all things and adorns them."[3]

Hence we learn these following particulars as to Confucian Cosmogony from Choo-tsze; 1st. The Great Origin of all things is God inherent in Matter; 2nd. God, therefore, pervades every portion of the entire Universe; 3rd. "Fate" is one of the names of God; and 4th. The Air which is the material origin of all things, is not the mere element so called, but Air animated by a Divine Principle, which he designates 神 or God. As this God or Fate is a perfect indivisible Unity, (as we shall see further on) it is evident that

---
1. 性理大全 Sec. ii, pp. 23, 24: xl, p. 24.
2. Works of the Two Chings, Vol. i, p. 52.
3. Yih King, Vol. xiv, 17, 15. Imp. Ed.

the Confucianists are Monotheists, while, at the same time, they are Pantheists, as their one God (神) pervades the entire Universe and all it's parts, and is the soul of each.

All the Pagan philosophers made God (Θεος, Deus) inherent in Eternal Matter the Great Origin of all things; so that "God penetrates, pervades, and animates matter," and is "the Divine Reason¹ inherent in the whole universe and all it's parts." Seneca says, "You mention Nature,² Fate, Fortune; names of this kind are all names of God (Dei) variously employing his power." "The Air of Anaximenes is a subtile ether animated with a Divine principle, whence it becomes the origin of all beings."³ "When Anaximenes speaks of Air, as when Thales speaks of Water, we must not understand these elements as they appear in this or that determined form on Earth, but as Water and Air pregnant with vital energy, and capable of infinite transmutations."⁴

In this "Fate" of Choo-tsze then, we have the God (Θεος, Deus) $κατ'$ $εξοχην$ of the Western philosophers, and the God $κατ'$ $εξοχην$ (至 神) of the Yih King.

(2, 3.) As Choo-tsze here states that the eternal Primordial Matter was generated by Fate or God, so also in the West, Matter, although considered to be eternal, was yet held by many to have been generated by the Deity. It is stated, for instance, in the Timœus (Ch. ix.) that the Universe was generated by its "Creator and Father;" and Plato is supposed to have followed Hermes and the Egyptians in thus holding that "the matter of all things emanated from the Deity or divine nature itself."⁵

The title "Nature" here given to Fate or God, sometimes includes the Primordial Air in which He is always inherent; "Nature is Fate;" "when we speak of Nature, we include the Air."⁶ Yet, Choo-tsze warns his disciples not to confound these two together, for this designation is only given to the Primordial Air in consequence of the *Melior Natura*, or God, who is inherent in it; he says, ... "Yet if we *always* consider the Air to be Nature, and Nature to be the Air, we do not clearly understand the subject."⁷ The "Nature" of the Confucianists therefore is precisely the "Natura" of the Stoics; and both schools designate the Divine Principle "Reason." "The Stoics divide nature into two parts; one, that which works; the other, that which offers itself to be wrought upon. In the former is the power of acting, in the latter is simple matter, nor is one able to do any thing without the other. Thus under one term of nature, they comprehend two things very diverse, God and the world, the artificer and the work, and they say that one cannot do without the other, as if nature were God mixed up with the world. For sometimes they so confound things, that God becomes the very soul of the world, and the world the body of God."⁸ "What is natura, says Seneca, but God the Divine Reason inherent in the whole universe and in all its parts? Or, you may call him if you please, the Author of all things."⁹

(4, 5.) Choo-tsze having explained to his pupils that the Great Origin of all things is Fate or God (神) inherent in the Primordial Matter, or the Infinite, Eternal, mass of Air from which all things are generated; one of those present propounds a question

---

1. See par. 24. Also, Enf. Hist. Philos. Vol. i. p. 334.
2. See par. 2, 3, and 24. Also, Cud. Intell. Syst. Vol i. p. 249 note.
3. Enf. Vol. i. p. 158.
4. Lewes's Hist. Philos. Vol. i. p. 9 note.
5. Cud. i. 570 note. Jowett's Plato. Vol. ii, pp. 523-4.
6. "Great Extreme," paragraph 17. Choo-tsze's works, Sec. xliii, p. 2.
7. Choo-tsze's Works, ch. xliii, p. 10.
8. Cud. i. 196, note.
9. Enf. i. 334.

NOTES. 127

to the Philosopher, as to which of these the priority in point of time is to be assigned. To this question there are two replies given by Choo-tsze, viz: 1st. That although we must not consider the one to be prior to the other in point of time, both being equally eternal, yet Fate or God being Incorporeal has in this respect priority over the Matter in which He is inherent, and which is a Corporeal and Material mass ; and 2nd. When we treat of the origin of these two, Fate or God has the decided priority, being self-existent, while the Primordial Matter is generated by or emanates from Him. "Fate generated the Air."[1]

Hence while these two are eternally united together, and can never exist separately from each other, they are nevertheless totally distinct Principles ; and thus, although God is not superior to Matter *in time*, He most decidedly is so *by nature*. This was precisely the doctrine held by Probus, Simplicius, and all the latter Platonists.[2]

(6.) This Great Origin of all things, or God inherent in Matter, is expressed in numbers, in the Yih King, by 1 or Monad. The inherent Fate or God is an Indivisible Unity, and the Infinite Primordial Air in which this Principle is inherent, is the material portion of Unity, that is to say Monad (太一) which divides into the several parts of the Universe. Hence the arranged Kosmos regarded as one whole, is designated Fate or God, and God is inherent in all its parts, even down to the meanest insect. Hence also, Man's soul or Principle of life is Fate, or God 神 Himself.[3]

In the Orphic verses " the whole world is represented as one great animal, God being the soul thereof."[4]

The Stoics used the designation "Fate" as one of the names of God Himself.[5] Also, according to these latter Philosophers, "Since the active principle of nature is comprehended within the world, and with matter makes one whole, it necessarily follows that God penetrates, pervades, and animates matter, and the things which are formed from it ; or, in other words, that he is the soul of the Universe." They further held that the soul of Man is a portion of the Divinity inherent in the Universe, which they regarded as "one Great Whole."[6]

(7.) The eternity of Motion here propounded is a well known tenet in Philosophy. Aristotle held the Motion of the first sphere or *Primum Mobile*, to be "without beginning, middle or end."[7]

In order to understand the statements made in this paragraph, we must refer to the first sentence in the Yih King to which Classic Choo-tsze constantly refers as his authority for the doctrines which he inculcates. The Universe moves round in a never ending circle, and the Yih King[8] divides this "*Khëen*" or animated Kosmos into four parts, thus:

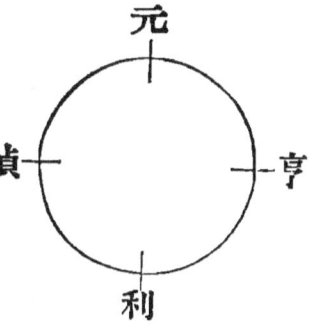

1. 性理大全 Sec. xxx, p. 10.
2. Cud. 1, 302 note.
3. "Dominans ille in nobis Deus." Cic. See below pp. 20, 26, 35, and "Great Extreme" par. 11.
4. Cud. 1. 507.   5. Ibid. p. 196. note.   6. Enf. 1, 332, 334, 351.   7. Enf, 1. 280.
8. Khëen Diagram.

This Circle represents the perpetual course in which the Kosmos revolves. At *Yuen* all things come forth, as for instance in the Spring season of the year; and at *Ching* they decay, as in Winter, only, however, to break forth into renewed life on again reaching the point *Yuen*. Hence Choo-tsze holds that "there is no termination to the present state of things," the eternal Universe and all its parts perpetually moving in an endless circle. From *Yuen* to the termination of *Hăng* at *Le*, is the place of Motion in which things spring forth, grow, and flourish; and from *Le* to the termination of *Ching* at *Yuen*, is the place of Rest or *vis inertiæ*, in which things decay and die. Hence all Motion is preceded by Rest and Rest is always followed by Motion in a perpetual circle, so that Motion and Rest are both eternal. The "opening and shutting" of the Kosmos refers to the Greater Revolutions of the Universe, which are compared in the Yih King to the opening and shutting of a door. This doctrine of the endless succession of similar worlds will come under notice in the division of this chapter which treats of Heaven and Earth. The designation "Great Extreme" is treated of in the third division, and the Light and Darkness into which the Primordial Air divides, in the fourth and last division.

(8.) Man, as well as the other parts of the Kosmos, is formed from the Primordial Air, and the inherent Fate or God (神) then becomes his soul as well as the soul or animating Principle of every other portion of the One Great Whole. One of the Philosopher's pupils now asks, where was this Fate or God before Man was generated as a body in which He could exist and act? Choo-tsze replies that this animating Principle of the Universe existed before any portion of it was, as it were, decerpt in order to form the soul in Man; just as the sea exists before any water is taken out of it. As each thing comes into existence, it receives a portion of this Divinity as its animating Principle; and it is the same Principle which is inherent in each. Yet, adds Choo-tsze, God (神) or the Divinity within me, is the Host while I am but his guest, being only united with him for a time; for, He is Eternal and Self-existent, while my body in which He dwells is mortal, and therefore subject to decay.

(9.) The Kosmos in which Fate or God is inherent, like the body in Man, is subject to decay. It is alternately in a Chaotic, and in an arranged state. Choo-tsze is now asked how Fate or God (神), being invisible, manifests His presence in the Primordial Air; to which he replies, that the chief portions of the Universe are preserved by Him from utter destruction while in Chaos, so that in due time a new Kosmos springs forth from the materials of the old one. Hence the Phœnix is used to represent the succession of worlds. That this tenet of an animated Universe is not confined to the Philosophers in China, is plain from the common phrase 活天活地 "Living Heaven and Earth," used every where throughout the Empire, and by all classes.

Zeno also held in common with all the Philosophers of antiquity that the Universe is οὐσία ἔμψυχος καὶ αισθητικὴ a sentient and animated being.[1] "All the theogonies make an eternal chaos the origin of all things."[2] This eternal Chaos is merely a Man, and thus every Pagan System commences from the First Man in his Mundane or deified character, whose soul is the Deity Himself, "Anterior to all of them (Gods, Goddesses and Demi-gods) the primordial matter or *person*, was chaos."[3] And Chinese history states that: "It is also handed down from antiquity, that the first to appear

---

1. Enf. 1, 835.   2. Ibid. p. 129.
3. Grote's Plato, Vol. 1, p. 3.

in the world was Pwan-koo *who is also called Chaos.*"[1] The Chaos therefore of the Confucianists, or the Eternal Primordial Air, is merely the first Man, who is deified by making the Deity Himself, (Fate or God 神), his soul.

(10.) The Eternal Primordial Air is the seed of the Universe, and being animated by the inherent Fate or God (神), possesses the power of generating every portion of the Kosmos from its own substance.[2] If God (神) were not inherent in this Air, it would then be merely inert matter, incapable of effecting any thing; and if the Primordial Air did not exist, then God could effect nothing, being in want of a medium through which to act. This Primordial Air (or Pwan koo) is designated 天 Heaven, in the Chinese classics, and 上帝 Shang-te, The (First or) Supreme Emperor; "Heaven is the accumulated Air."[3] "When Heaven produces and completes the myriad of things, and rules and governs them, the title given to that Being is Te."[4] *i. e.* Shang-te. Shang-te therefore is the arranged Primordial Air, that is to say, the kosmos or *second* God who generates all things from and within himself, and who owes all his powers as well as his existence to the First God, viz. Fate. Aristotle states that Anaximenes also regarded his Primordial Air as God, that is to say, as Heaven or Jupiter. In fact, the Primordial Matter was considered by all philosophers to be Infinite, Eternal, and Divine; the more ethereal portion of it being regarded as the Governor and Ruler of the whole mass, and consequently of all things made from it.[5]

Fate or God (神) inherent in the Primordial Air is also the Infinite Vacuum which surrounds the formed Kosmos, and in which the latter revolves; "a pure, empty wide world," the only Incorporeal Principle in the Universe. This is the "Reason" of the Yih King; "Reason is the Great Vacuum and is Incorporeal.[6] "This Principle (Fate or God) is so great that it comprehends Heaven and Earth, and is the support of generation and transmutation; so minute, that it enters into every fibre and particle; there is no distance which it cannot traverse, and there is nothing so mean that it does not reach it; yet we must discern what it is which thus pervades all things."[7]

In this we have a further proof that the Confucianist Fate or God (神) is the Θεος κατ' εξοχην of the West; Philo held that "God is that space which surrounds and encompasses the whole nature of things."[8] Onatus the Pythagorean says, "It seemeth to me that there is not only one God, but that there is one the greatest and highest God that governeth the whole world......That is that God who contains and comprehends the whole world."[9] According to the Stoics, the Infinite Vacuum which surrounds the Kosmos is the only thing which is really Incorporeal.[10] "If space be not made or created, then it will be nothing else than the divine immensity or God Himself."[11] Diogenes Laertius states that the Stoical doctrine on this point was, "that without the world an immense vacuum is circumfused which is incorporeal: and that that is incorporeal which can be contained by bodies, but is not contained." Philo also held "that God is that space, so to speak, in which bodies exist and revolve, and which penetrates and pervades all things."[12]

Fate or the Incorporeal Reason, then, is the First God in the Confucian system and

---

1. 綱鑑會集 Vol. i. p. 2, 5.   2. See also par. 12.
3. See below "Heaven and Earth" par. 39.   4. Legges "Notions," &c. p. 12.
5. Cud. i, 161, 184, 186. See below, par. 22.   6. 性理 &c. Vol. xii, p. 1.
7. Choo-tze's, Works, Ch. xli, 15 : xlvi, 12.
8. Cud. iii, 242. note.   9. Ibid. i, 374.   10. Enf. i, 332.   11. Cud. ii, 515. note.
12. Ibid. iii, 231 note; 242 note.

Shang-te or Heaven, the animated Primordial Air is the second God or the Demiurgus, who grows up, as it were, from Chaos into the fully arranged Kosmos. The Hermaic books state that "The world is a second God." "God is the father of the world, and the world is the son of God." "This whole world is a great God and the image of a greater."[1]

(11, 12, 13.) Fate or God is superior to the Infinite Primordial Air by nature, but is not prior *in time*, both being equally eternal. But, the very existence of the whole Kosmos and each part of it, entirely depends upon the inherent Fate or God (神). The Primordial Air, which is Heaven or *Shang-te*, receives his animation and power to act as the Demiurge, in generating, nourishing and pervading all things, from the supreme Fate or God (神) who is his animating soul, and without which he could have no existence. Fate or God is the only "Incorporeal substance" in the Universe and both He and the Primordial Air which he surrounds and also pervades, are equally Infinite and Eternal. God (神) is Infinite as to space, and Heaven or *Shang-te* is Infinite as to his parts or portions into which he divides.

(14, 15.) "The Great Framer" is a title of the Demiurgus Heaven or *Shang-te*, from whose ethereal substance all things are made, and in which each is again absorbed at death, as in the case of the Western Kronos or "devouring Jupiter."

(16, 17.) When Heaven or *Shang-te* breathes forth his Air, then all things exist and flourish; but when he draws in his breath they all die being deprived of their animating principle. This *Shang-te*, however, so frequently mentioned in the Classics, is not a personal being dwelling in the heavens, but is Heaven itself animated by an inherent soul called Fate or God who is the real source of all happiness and misery. *Shang-te* or Heaven is merely the revolving Primordial Air, or the Kosmos, which is sometimes arranged, and sometimes in a state of Chaos, when all things return to his bosom. Chaos or "decline," and the arranged Kosmos or "fulness," follow each other *ad infinitum.*

(18.) Fate or God (神) being eternally united with the Primordial Air or *Shang-te*, acts through the latter, who is therefore merely the Demiurgic Framer and Ruler of the Kosmos, and could not exist without this soul which dwells within him.

(19.) The Seasons in this system are not mere states of the atmosphere, but are animated beings, portions of the one Primordial Air or *Shang-te*, and hence they are sacrificed to. They are each animated by the one Fate or God (神) which pervades all things. Hence these Gods are precisely such as the Gods of Anaximenes were, for, "Anaximenes made infinite Air to be the first original and cause of all things; and yet was he not therefore silent concerning the gods, much less did he deny them; nevertheless he did not believe the air to have been made by the gods, but the gods to have been *all generated out of the air.*"[2] These "Four Airs" or portions of Heaven or *Shang-te*, Confucius thus describes: "The lofty azure vault is Heaven (*i. e. Shang-te*); the Spring is 蒼天 (上帝); the summer is 昊天 (上帝); the Autumn is 旻天 (上帝); and the Winter is 上天 (上帝).[3] Hence *Shang-te* or Heaven, like Jupiter or Heaven, is both the father and ruler of the Gods, as well as of Men.

(20.) In this paragraph Choo-tsze refers to the numbers of the Yih King.[4] The Primordial Air which is Heaven or *Shang-te*, is "The Great Monad" (太一) or

---

1. Cud. i. 560. 2. Cud. i, 389.
3. 爾雅 Sec. 中. Ch. viii, p. 20. 4 Bk. III. Ch. ix.

number 1, who, like his counterpart the Monad Jupiter, generates the world from his own substance, by his own gyrations; *e. gr.* "Hence Rites and Ceremonies derive their origin from the Great Monad (*i.e. Shang-te*), who *dividing* became Heaven and Earth; *gyrating*, became Light and Darkness; *transmuting*, became the Four Seasons; and *separating orderly* became the Demon-gods (鬼神),"[1] &c.

The Confucian Monad then, is the Primordial Air which is animated by the inherent Fate or God (神), who, although He pervades all things is yet an Indivisible Unity;[2] and hence the numbers of the Yih King are animated Beings. Pythagoras also held that "Numbers were Beings:" he believed that "numbers were things in reality, not merely in symbol:" and, Aristotle states that "the Pythagoreans did not separate Numbers from Things. They held Number to be the Principle and Material of things, no less than their essence and power." "The primary Being according to Anaximander is unquestionably a Unity. It is One yet All. It comprises within itself the multiplicity of elements from which all mundane things are composed; and these elements only need to be separated from it to appear as separate phenomena of nature. Creation is the decomposition of the Infinite. How does this decomposition originate? By the eternal motion which is the condition of the Infinite,"[3] &c.

As all the inferior Gods are parts of *Shang-te* or the Primordial Air, they are all equally *Shang-te*; *e. gr.* 上帝即天也聚天之神而言之則謂之上帝. "Shang-te is Heaven; all the Gods of Heaven collectively are *Shang-te*."[4] That is, Heaven or *Shang-te* is "one God yet all Gods," and like his counterpart Heaven or Jupiter, might thus address the other deities:—

"Cœlicolæ, mea membra, Dei; quos nostra potestas
Officiis divisa facit."[5]

Hence *Shang-te* is a mere compound of creatures worshipped as a Creator.

(21.) Man, as well as the Kosmos or *Shang-te*, is made from the Primordial Air; and the Air within a Man, and which constitutes his twofold soul, is precisely the same as that without him. Thus the Confucianists seem to have gone through the same process of reasoning as the Philosopher Anaximenes, whose ideas are thus represented by Lewes:[6] "His life he believed to be Air. Was there not also without him no less than within him, an ever-moving, ever-present, invisible Air? The Air which was within him, and which he called Life, was it not a part of the Air which was without? And if so, was not this Air the Beginning of things? He looked arround him and thought his conjecture was confirmed. The Air seemed universal. The Earth was as a broad leaf resting upon it. All things were produced from it; all things were resolved into it. When he breathed, he drew in a part of the universal life. All things were nourished by Air, as he was nourished by it." Diogenes of Apollonia held that the Air is "a soul, and therefore it is living and intelligent."[7] "Form is the habitation of Life, Air (氣) is the Origin of Life."[8]

(22.) The Infinite Primordial Air is an Intelligent Being or Animal, which, in virtue of it's union with the Eternal Fate or God (神), is endowed with the powers of understanding and sensation. These powers are conferred upon the spiritual portion

---

1. Le Ke, sec. iv. 禮運.
2. See "Great Extreme," 11 and 37.
3. Lewes, i, 16, 30, 31.
4. Le Ke, sec. v, chapter xi. Com.
5. Ond, ii, 206.
6. Vol. i, p. 9.
7. Lewes, Vol. i, 10, 11.
8. Kang-he.

of the Air, that is to say, the most subtile Ether. Thus the Primordial Air, or Heaven, or *Shang-te*, is a compound Being or Animal; the visible Heaven (including the Earth) being his body (體) and the subtile Ether being his rational soul, which is made to be a rational soul by the inherent Fate or Reason or God (神); and hence this soul is called 天之神 the God (or rational soul) of Heaven or *Shang-te*. All the Confucianist Gods, in fact, are souls. The usual designation of this subtile Ether or rational soul is "Mind," the Νους or Mens of the Western philosophers. It is plain then—1. That Chaos consists of Mind inherent in grosser Matter; and 2. That this Mind or Demiurgus is only the *second* God. "If there were no Air, then Fate would not have any thing to rest upon."[1] This "Air," Choo-tsze also designates "Mind (心);" "If there were no Mind, then Fate would not have any thing to rest upon."[2] This is the "Νους κάντων βασιλεὺς," "Mind, the King of all things" of Plato; or his "one archetypal Mind, the Demiurgus;" and this mind he held to be eternal yet generated by the First God whom he calls τ'αγαθον.[3] "Mind," (*i. e.* Jupiter), "says Macrobius was begotten from that God who is truly supreme."[4] Archytas in his book of principles says that "There must be something better than Mind; and this thing better than Mind, is that which we (properly) call God."[5]

(23, 24.) Man and *Shang-te* or the Kosmos are precisely the same, both being made from exactly the same Principles. Hence Heaven or *Shang-te* is merely "a Great Man," and Man is "a little Heaven" or *Shang-te*, or Microcosm. Hence also the soul in both is the same, viz., Incorporeal Reason or God (神). And as in the World, so also in Man, this First God unites with his "Mind" and makes it to be a rational soul; and hence the latter is, in the Classics styled God (神), or the Divinity within us.

"Man, according to the Stoics, is an image of the world; one whole composed of body and Mind. The mind of man is a spark of that Divine fire, which is the soul of the world. That Eternal Reason by which all nature is animated, and which by its productive power, communicates essential qualities to every thing that exists, impressed the forms, qualities, and powers of man, upon certain portions of matter. The soul of man being a portion of the Deity, is then of *the same nature;* a subtile fiery substance, endued with intelligence and reason; but the energy of this principle is confined and constrained in the birth of man, by its union with grosser matter."[6]

(25.) The "Fate" of each thing existing first, before the thing itself has any substantial form, refers to what Choo-tsze states in par. 10, where he defines Fate or God to be the Great Vacuum which surrounds the Kosmos. In this Fate or Vacuum are contained all the 象 or Ideas (意想; see Kang-he) of things before they obtain form by union with a portion of the Primordial Air.

(26.) Fate or God (神), who is the "Incorporeal Reason" of the Yih King, must have an ethereal vehicle to rest in. Abstract Reason can do nothing of itself, no more than abstract Matter can. Join both together and Matter becomes animated and capable of action, while the inherent Divine Reason makes it to be a rational animal. Deprive Man's soul of this Divine Reason or God (神) and it ceases to be an intelligent Mind; separate the Divine Reason from the soul and the former has no medium through which to act, for God can do nothing without Matter. This eternity of Matter was, in

---

1. See above, par. 5.   2. Works, ch. xliv, 2 : " Heaven and Earth," par. 29.
3. Cud. ii, 89, 868.   4. Cud. ii, 163. Compare above par. 2.
5. Ibid. p 53.   6. Enf. 1, 342. See below, par. 27.

fact, the doctrine of all antiquity. "All philosophers," says Gassendi, "agree in the pre-existence of the matter of which the universe is composed, because nothing can be produced from nothing; whereas however, Scripture truth declares that the universe was created out of nothing and from no material."[1] The smallest insect, Choo-tsze states, is made from the same primordial Air as Heaven or *Shang-te* and Man, and the same inherent Principle (Fate or Reason or God) animates all. This is Pantheism and Monotheism combined.

(27.) The origin of evil Choo-tsze derives from the vitiation of the Primordial Air. The inherent Principle or God animates every thing made from this Primordial Air, but the latter becomes more and more deteriorated as it gets further from the Original Fountain. Hence Choo-tsze states elsewhere that sheep and horses only differ from men, in that the Air of which they are made is much grosser in them than it is in Man, and therefore the Divine Reason which animates them cannot act perfectly through this imperfect medium.[2] That is to say, Fate resembles pure water which may be muddied although it still remains water.[3]

(28.) The "Great Extreme" of the Yih King is fully explained in the next division of the chapter. The "Two E" generated by it are merely the division of the Primordial Air into two kinds, in order to form the Kosmos and generate "the Myriad of things." Laou-tsze evidently held that the union between the Divine Reason and the Primordial Air (which is the Great Monad or *Shang-te*) is not absolutely necessary to the existence of the former, whereas the Confucianists hold, that this union is as necessary and as intimate as that of the body and soul in Man. Although the Confucianists hold that the Primordial Air is generated by God (神) or the Divine Reason,[4] yet they deny that the latter has any priority *in point of time* over the former; whereas Laou-tsze does give a certain priority in point of time to the Divine Reason; e. gr. "Reason is prior (先) to *Shang-te*"[5] (i. e. The Great Monad).

(30.) The designation here given by Choo-tsze to Fate or God (神), is one which Plato also gives to his Supreme Θεος, viz., "the Adorner." This title Choo-tsze takes from the Yih King.[6]

(31.) The compound "Fate inherent in Air" must be viewed under a twofold aspect, 1° As the Great Fountain from which all things are made; and 2° As to the proportion (as it were) in which each is "received" by the various parts of creation. In Man, for instance, this Fate is predominant, and hence he is the most intelligent of all creatures; while in brutes, and in the vegetable creation, the Air or material principle predominates, and hence the action of the Incorporeal Principle which animates them is obstructed. The material principle is also capable of being vitiated, and this vitiation still further obstructs the free action of the superior principle, or "The Divinity which stirs within us."

(32, 33.) When the Light shines in through a window, it falls upon various objects in the room. Falling upon dark objects it appears more dull than when it falls upon white objects such as paper, &c., yet the Light is but one light. So also the Divine Fate or Reason which is the soul of all things, when it animates a sheep, or a cow, or an ant, appears comparatively dull; whereas when it animates Man it shines forth in

---

1. Cnd. iii, 144. 2. See below, p. 32. 3. See par. 33.
4. See above, par. 2, 4. 5. 道德經 ch. iv. 6. Bk. iv. 說卦 ch. vi.

full intelligence. Yet this Divine Principle, the soul of each alike, is one and the same. He resembles pure Light which may be dulled, and pure water which may be muddied.

(34.) Here we have another appellation, given in the Yih King to the Confucianist Fate or God (神) and which proves Him to be the $\theta\epsilon o\varsigma$ $\kappa a\tau'$ $\epsilon\xi o\chi\eta\nu$ of Plato and other philosophers in the West, viz. "The Good" ($\tau'a\gamma a\theta o\nu$).[1]

(35.) The twofold soul in Man and in the rest of creation, is Air; the "Nature" of each is the Divine Principle which pervades all alike. Hence when this Air, which is the soul, disperses at death, the being ceases to exist, the soul returning to the entire mass of primordial Air (or "Heaven") from which it originally came.

(36.) The Eternal Fate or God (神) is the First Mover, and the Primordial Air, or Great Monad, or *Shang-te*, depends upon Him for the power of Motion and also *vis inertiæ*. In this we have further proof that this "Fate" of the Confucianists is the "Fate" of the Stoics; that is to say, their Supreme God (神, $\Theta\epsilon o\varsigma$ Deus). "The essence of the First Mover is different from that of corporeal substances; indivisible, because unity is perfect; immutable, because nothing can change itself, and eternal because motion itself is eternal. This power is an incorporeal Intelligence, happy in the contemplation of himself; the first cause of all motion, and in fine, the Being of beings, or God."[2]

---

1. Yih King, bk. iii, ch. v.()   2. Enf. i, 284.

THE GREAT EXTREME.

The previous section treats of animated Chaos, or the Eternal, Infinite, Primordial Matter or Air as one dark mass, in which the Eternal, Self-existent Fate or God is inherent. In this section the Primordial Air is treated of as divided into two Airs, in order to the formation of the complete Kosmos. These two portions are respectively designated 陽 Yang or Light, the subtile Ether or Mind, the *Linga* of the Hindoos; and 陰 Yin or Darkness, the grosser Air, and the *Yoni* of the Hindoos. These are the "Two E" of the Yih King, the former being designated 乾 Khēen and the latter 坤 Khwăn, in that Classic. The animating soul, which in Chaos is designated Fate, is now designated "The great Extreme." The following figures will assist the student to obtain a clear idea of the statements made in this section:

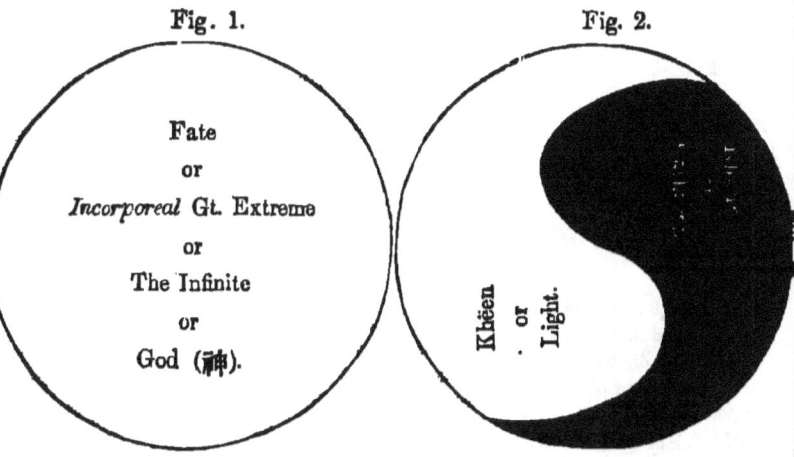

Fig. 2. is the divided Air (氣) or *Corporeal* Great Extreme, and must be supposed to be placed over Fig. 1. in order to represent the twofold Air in which "Fate" is inherent. See plate III, fig. 4, also plate II.

(Paragraphs 1, 2, 3, 4.) In the first paragraph Choo-tsze tells us that Fate or God is the Great Extreme, and in par. 3 that the Primordial Air is the Great Extreme; this designation therefore like that of "Nature," includes both the Immaterial Principle or God, and the Eternal Matter from which He makes the Universe. Hence as in the case of "Nature" we are distinctly told that the designation "Great Extreme" is only given to the Matter or Kosmos in consequence of the inherent Divine Principle or God; *e. gr.* "(The Great Extreme) is *Khēen* and *Khwăn*, (Fig. 2. above) united in one. Because of it's one God (神 Fig. 1.) it is called the Great Extreme; because of its two

136 NOTES.

transmutations (twofold Air) it is called the Two E."¹ (Fig. 2.) There is but One God (神) in the whole Universe, of which latter He is the animating soul; and lest He should be confounded with Matter or the Kosmos, the Chinese Philosophers commonly designate Him "The Infinite" (fig. 1.) and retain the designation "Great Extreme" for the Primordial Matter (fig. 2.), intimating the inseparable union between the two by placing the conjunction " 而 and," between them, thus, "The Infinite *and* The Great Extreme,"² which is a periphrasis for the animated Κοσμος.

In Chaos, Fate or God not only surrounds the entire mass of Primordial Air but is inherent in it, and pervades it; and in the fully completed Kosmos, made from this Air, this Fate or God, now designated "The Great Extreme" is inherent in each of its parts. He occupies the centre pivot on which the Kosmos revolves, and His influence extends throughout the whole circle. He also occupies the centre of each portion of the Universe.

When this inherent Fate or Great Extreme or God communicates the power of Motion to the Primordial Air (par. 36, previous section), he acts chiefly upon the Light or more subtile portion. The Darkness is the coarser portion and possesses the *vis inertiæ*. And, as the Primordial Air is eternal, so the Light and Darkness into which it divides, as well as the Motion of the former and the Rest of the latter are all equally eternal.

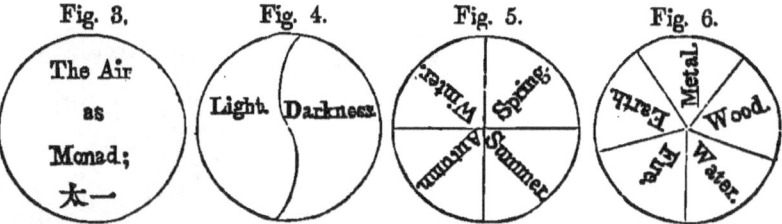

Circle 3 represents the whole body of Primordial Air; 4 represents this *same* circle divided into two (a male and a female *soul*) in order to generate all things; 5 represents it divided into the Four Seasons; and 6 into the Five Elements. After this, the same body of Air scattering further becomes all things; so "The One" is also "All Things." Fate or the Immaterial Great Extreme, viz., "The Infinite" or God (神), is inherent in the Monad and in each of its divisions. And as the whole body of Air is *Shang-te*, so are the two divisions *Shang-te*, the four divisions are *Shang-te* (see preceding sec. par. 19 and note), and the five divisions are *Shang-te*. In the Classics the last are called "The Five Rulers" or *Shang-tes* and are sacrificed to separately.³ The soul of each division of the Air is the one Indivisible Fate or God (神) inherent in the Kosmos and each of its divisions or parts.

Plato held that the Kosmos "is one animated being, including within its limits all animated natures;" that "from perfect parts one perfect whole was produced, of a *spherical figure*, as most beautiful in itself," &c.: and, "that the soul (Θεος) which pervades this sphere is the cause of its revolution round its centre,"⁴ &c.

1. Yih King, bk. iii, ch. xi, (Imp. Ed.). 2. See below par. 13, 14.
3. Le Ke, sec. iii. 4. Enf. 1, 237, 238. Jowett, ii, 586, 527-8.

NOTE. 137

As the Primordial Air is generated by Fate or God (神) it follows that the Kosmos (or *Shang-te*) formed from that Air, is only the *second* God (神); so also Cicero, speaking of the Universe, says, "Thus that eternal God, procreated this perfectly happy god (*deum*), the world."[1] So also Plato.[2] The Kosmos Jupiter or Heaven, like the Kosmos *Shang-te* or Heaven, was Androgynous.[3] And, as the Confucianists hold that their one 神 or First God is part of a spherical Universe; so also did the Stoics, concerning their one $\theta\epsilon o\varsigma$ or Deus or First God.[4]

(5, 6, 7.) The designation "Great Extreme" is given both to the Fate or God inherent in the twofold Primordial Matter, and also to the Matter itself divided into Light and Darkness. Hence in the Yih King, this inherent God (神) is said to be "Incomprehensible" because, as a perfect Unity he is in both the Light and the Darkness, (including the entire series made from each), whole and entire, without division of substance.[5] This First God is also designated "Reason" (道) and "Incorporeal Reason" in the same Classic.

All things are generated by the animated Primordial Air or Heaven or *Shang-te*, by his constant gyrations; but he owes all his powers of Motion, &c., as well as his very existence to his inherent Soul, the Immaterial Great Extreme or Fate or First God (神). In fact he would "turn upside down," but for the presence of this preserving Power.

(8, 9.) Choo-tsze, in these paragraphs, explains the Confucianist idea as to the eternity of Light and Darkness, Motion and Rest. The animated Heaven or material Great Extreme or *Shang-te*, perpetually revolves producing the Light and the Darkness, which are animated beings in virtue of the inherent Deity.

(10.) From Chaos, or God inherent in Matter, to the full arrangement of that Matter into the complete Kosmos, this animated Universe is to be regarded as One Whole Animal or Being, viz. 太一 or the Great Monad *Shang-te*, who, as a great Hermaphrodite, generates all things from his own substance (Air), and within himself.

(11.) In this paragraph we have another striking proof that the First God of the Yih King is the same as the First God of the Western Philosophers. The Great Extreme or Fate or God is a perfect indivisible Unity which pervades all things without division of substance, just as the Moon is seen whole and entire in each river and canal without being divided into several Moons.[6] As the designation "The Great Extreme" includes both Fate or God, and the Matter or Air in which he is inherent, one of Choo-tsze's disciples asks him, to which portion of the Great Origin of all things he refers when he speaks of the Great Extreme being an indivisible Unity—to Fate (or God), or to the Primordial Matter (or Air)? To which the Philosopher replies that his statement refers to Fate, or the Immaterial Principle, which, as we have seen, he himself calls God (神).[7] This is the 至神 or First God of the Classics and the title given to him, viz., "The Adorner of all things" is used by the Confucianists to distinguish Him from the second god or *Shang-te* who is the twofold Air and is styled "Demon-god" (鬼神). Hence Choo-tsze tells us when treating of the First God, that, "This God (神)

1. Cud. i, 389. 2. Cud. i, 376. Jowett, ii, 528. 3. Cud. i, 506.
4. Enf. I, 333. 5. Yih King, bk. iii, ch. v. (last par.).
6. See also par. 27, 37. 7. See "Fate and Air," par. 1, note.

is NOT the Demon-god (鬼 神), He is the God (神) who adorns all things."[1] The First God, Fate or Incorporeal Reason, is an Indivisible Unity; the second god is the Air or *Shang-te*, "The Great Monad," who divides into the various portions of the Universe; the First God being the one animating Soul of the whole and of each part. A plainer assertion of Monotheism and yet Pantheism, it would be difficult to find. "Heaven (*Shang-te*) divides and becomes Earth, Earth divides and becomes the myriad of things, but Reason (God) cannot be divided."[2] "Body is divisible but God (神) cannot be divided."[3] "God (神) is Unity; he rides upon the Air (*Shang-te* or Monad) and changes and transmutes it."[4]

This First God of the Yih King, therefore, is the first hypostasis of Plato and others, called by them τὸ ἓν Unity and τ' ἀγαθον Goodness itself (善 Yih King, sec. iii, ch. v.).[5]

So also Parmenides and Xenophanes "affirmed that the one or unity was the first principle of all; matter itself, as well as other things *being derived from it*; they meaning by this one, that highest or Supreme God who is over all."[6]

"It is necessary," says Lewes, "to caution the reader against the supposition that by the One God Xenophanes meant a Personal God distinct from the universe. He was a monotheist in contradistinction to his political contemporaries; but his monotheism was pantheism. Indeed this point would never have been doubted, notwithstanding the ambiguity of language, if moderns had steadily kept before their minds the conceptions held by the Greeks of their Gods as personifications of the powers of Nature. When Xenophanes argued against the Polytheism of his contemporaries, he argued against their personifying as distinct deities the various aspects of The One; he was wrath with their degradation of the divine nature by assimilating it to human nature, by making these powers *persons* and independent existences—conceptions irreconcileable with that of the unity of God. He was a monotheist therefore, but his monotheism was pantheism; he could not separate God from the world, which was merely the manifestation of God. He could not conceive God as the One Existent, and admit the existence of a world *not* God. There could be but One Existence with many modes, that one was God."[7]

The illustration given by Choo-tsze to prove the perfect Unity of God while pervading all things is remarkable. According to the doctrine of Emanation as held by Western Philosophers, God "is like a Sun pouring forth his rays, without losing any of its substance."[8]

(12.) The animated twofold Air, Heaven or *Shang-te*, when arranged out of Chaos, occupies the outer circle of the Kosmos, and enfolds it, preserving the world in existence by his constant gyrations.[9]

(13—18.) The Immaterial portion of the Great Extreme, viz. Fate or God, is designated "The Infinite," not only to express His Incorporeality, but also to prevent the possibility of His being confounded with the Primordial Air or *Shang-te* in which He is inherent, both these being included under the one title "The Great Extreme." In this we have an additional proof that this First God of the Confucianists (神), is

---

1. 性理, &c. sec. v, p. 81. 2. Ibid, sec. ii, p. 22. 3. Ibid, p. 34.
4. Ibid, sec. xi, p. 33. 5. Cud. i, 184–5, 601.
6. Cud. ii, 38. 7. Hist. Phil. i, 47.
8. Lewes, i, 398. 9. See below "Heaven and Earth," par. 2, and note.

NOTE. 139

the First God of Western Philosophers (Θεος; Deus); Melissus, for instance, affirmed that his "One Ens" was Incorporeal, and he designated Him "Infinite (ἄπειρον) to signify his eternity and incorruptibility."[1]

This First God or Incorporeal Great Extreme is "Omnipresent, Incorporeal, and Infinite." Motion and Rest are the properties of the Primordial Air or *Shang-te*, the Demiurge, and are produced by the power of the First God, but must not be confounded with Him. In par. 15 these two parts of the Great Extreme are carefully distinguished. The Active portion of the Primordial Air or *Shang-te*, possesses the power of Motion, bestowed upon it by the First God, who makes that subtile Ether His Hegemonikon; while *Shang-te's* inert or more material portion, his ethereal body in fact, possesses the *vis inertiæ*. This moving and resting *Shang-te* or Air, however, must not be mistaken for the First God or Immaterial portion of the Great Extreme who confers these powers upon him. *Shang-te* is the Second God or animated Kosmos, (body and soul) of the Western Philosophers—the "son" of the First God because generated by Him.

The 17th par. makes this distinction very clear. The designation "Great Extreme" includes God (神) and the arranged Kosmos in which He is inherent; the title "Nature" includes God (神) and the Primordial Air from which the Kosmos is formed; but, in neither case must the Matter be confounded with the *Melior Natura* inherent in it.

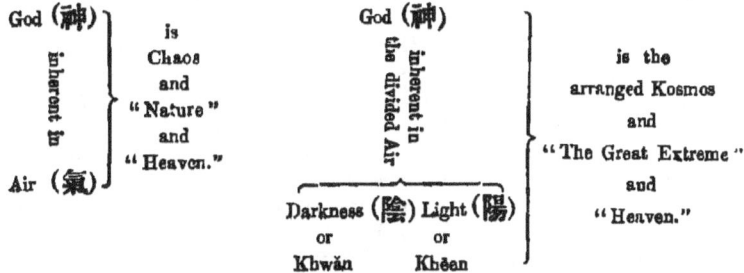

From the completed being "Heaven" or the Kosmos, Man receives his "Virtuous Nature," which is the Deity Himself (神) who is the "Incorporeal Reason" inherent in the Mind of the Kosmos or *Shang-te*, and also in the Mind of Man the lesser *Shang-te* or Microcosm; "making Mind to be Mind."[2] The title "The Good" (τ'αγαθον given in the Yih King) to the First God or the "Incorporeal Reason," has been already mentioned as the designation of the first divine "Hypostasis" of Plato's theology.

(19.) The description given in this paragraph of "The Great Extreme" or God, corresponds to that given of Him by the Egyptian Philosophers; e. gr. "Ammon in his books calleth God most hidden (πάγκρυφον), and Hermes plainly declareth that it is hard to conceive God, but impossible to express him."[3] "God (神) is not confined to place and is Omnipresent. He unites Himself to the Mind of Man, which thus has its origin in Unity. Reason and Unity are but forced names of God (神); if we

---

1. Cud. ii, 46, 47.
2. "Heaven and Earth," par. 20 : and previous Part, par. 22.
3. Cud. 1, 564.

consider God (神) to be God (神) that is the best appellation."[1] Hence Confucius says, "My Reason (道) is the all pervading Unity."[2] Hence the Sage was *Shang-te* or Heaven in human form.

According to the old Egyptian theology, God is said to have both no name and every name."[3]

(20, 21, 22.) The Great Extreme, and Fate, are both designations of the Supreme God, or the Incorporeal Vacuum which surrounds the Kosmos and thus "contains Motion and Rest." The proper designation of this, however, is, as we have seen, "The Infinite," while the animated Kosmos or *Shang-te* is "The Great Extreme." This latter Moves and Rests when divided into Light and Darkness; the Light being the part which has Motion, and the Darkness the part which has *vis inertiæ*. The Light or Ether is an Intellectual Mind or Soul; *made to be so* by the inherent Divine Reason; and this Reason inherent in Mind is The Great Extreme of the formed Kosmos. Hence God (神) as the soul of Chaos is called "Fate," while as the soul of the arranged Kosmos He is called "The Great Extreme," or more properly "The Infinite" or "Extremeless" (無極). "Leibnitz is of opinion that the Li (Fate) of the Chinese is the Chaotic soul of the world, and that their Taikie (Great Extreme) is the soul of the formed universe; in fine *the Deity of the Stoics*."[4] The First God (神) of the Confucianists then is identical with the First God (Θεος; Deus) of the Stoics.

(23, 24.) Fate or The Infinite (Incorporeal Great Extreme), or Nature, or God (神), rides upon the Primordial Air or Heaven or *Shang-te* "as a man rides upon a horse" and drives him at His will. This First God is inherent in all things, and is the extreme point or "Centre" of each. Hence His Hegemonikon in the Kosmos or Heaven or "Imperial *Shang-te*" is in the Centre, or the "Mind" of the Kosmos.[5] So also Plato held that the soul or Mind of the Kosmos was situated "in the centre," and was "stretched throughout its body in every direction—so as not only to reach the circumference, but also to enclose and wrap it round externally."[6] Plato also held, as Choo-tze does, that "Fate" is superior to the Demiurgus,[7] (Jupiter or "Imperial *Shang-te*.")

(25 and 30.) The material portion of The Great Extreme, that is to say, the Primordial Air arranged into the complete Kosmos, is a Great Numen, and a most Divine Animal or Being. The formation of this Kosmos is as follows; 1° There is one Self-existent God (神); 2° He generates the Eternal Primordial Air (see previous sec. par. 2), which He moulds from its Chaotic state into the arranged animated Kosmos. This Kosmos therefore, animated by "Mind" is the second god or "Imperial *Shang-te*" body and soul. So also Timœus Locrus "asserted one eternal and unmade God, the maker of the whole world, and besides this another generated god, *the world itself animated*, with its several parts."[6] "God willing to make the world the best that it was capable of, made it a generated god, such as should never be destroyed by any other cause but only by that God himself who framed it, if he should ever will to

---

1. 性理, &c. sec. xii, p. 3.
2. Lun Yu, bk. ii, sec. iv, (里仁) ch. xv.   3. Cud. ii, 259.
4. Enf. ii, 577. Also par. 9 of previous Part.
5. See Legge's Mencius p. 281, note.   6. Grote's Plato, Vol. iii, p. 254. Jowett, ii, 528.
7. Grote, iii, p. 249.   8. Cud. ii, 56.

destroy it.¹" "......he (the Supreme God) generated the world a blessed god (θεος)."² Choo-tsze (in par. 30) calls this Kosmos "a most Divine (至神) thing," in consequence of the inherent 至神. "The world," says Plinius Secundus, "and that which *by another name is called Heaven*, by whose circumgyration all things are governed, ought to be believed a Numen, eternal, immense, such as never was made, and shall never be destroyed."³ This second God or the world, was called by Anaximander (as by Choo-tsze) "τὸ θεῖον, the divinest thing of all."⁴ As Choo-tsze designates this animated Kosmos "Heaven," so does Plato, *e. gr.* "Let the Universe then be called Heaven, or the world, or by any other name which it usually receives."⁵ Hence Choo-tsze and the Western Philosophers, hold that there is one Eternal, Self-existent, Indivisible Unity or God, (神, Θεος, or Deus), who is the First God, by whom the second God, viz., "Heaven" (*Shang-te,* Ζευς, Jupiter) or the animated Kosmos is generated; and this latter is esteemed by them the highest Numen. According to Diogenes of Apollonia "the Universe is a living being, spontaneously evolving itself, deriving its transformation from its own vitality."⁶ According to Plato, a Demiurgus forms copies of Ideas or Forms out of chaos. "The Kosmos became animated, rational,—a God."⁷

(26.) In the formed Kosmos or Heaven, three distinct things are comprised in one whole, viz., 1 "Fate," or "Nature,"—the First God; 2 Mind, or the most subtile Ether; and 3, the remainder of the Primordial Air, the ethereal body of "Mind." The second of these is *Shang-te* or The Great Extreme of the formed world. Compared with Fate or the First God, *Shang-te* or Mind is non-Ens or Matter; while compared with his more material aerial vehicle, the grosser Air, he cannot be said to be non-Ens, for, he animates it, and is therefore spiritual compared with it. Hence Choo-tsze says elsewhere, that "Mind compared with Nature (*i. e.* Fate) is more material; compared with the Air, he is certainly more spiritual."⁸ This grosser portion of the Primordial Matter is called non-Ens (無) in par. 30. Hence the First God, who is above Mind or the Demiurgus, is the only real Ens in the Kosmos, and compared to Him the Kosmos itself or animated *Shang-te* is non-Ens, and is always changing its form, owing to the endless succession of worlds. Plato also, who made Fate superior to the Demiurgus or Mind, distinguishes in his Timœus between "1 Ens or the Existent, the eternal and unchangeable, the world of Ideas and Forms apprehended only by mental conception or Reason, but the object of infallible cognition. 2 The Generated and Perishable—the sensible, phenomenal, material world—which never really exists, but is always appearing and disappearing." The animated Kosmos, according to Plato, belongs to the last.⁹

(27—30.) The Great Extreme is Fate or God inherent in the Primordial Air. When it is said that "Reason is the Great Extreme" the self-existent Fate or God is referred to; while in the phrase "Mind is the Great Extreme" the subtile Primordial Air (or *Shang-te*) is referred to, which is made to be a "Mind" and is constituted the Lord of the entire body by the inherent Fate or Reason or God (神), whose proper title is "The Infinite" or Extremeless.

(31, 32.) The Primordial Air or *Shang-te* depends upon his inherent Reason or

1. Cud. ii, 55.   2. Timœus, sec. 13. Jowett, ii, 528.   3. Cud. i, 210.
4. Ibid, ii, 49. 5. Timœus, sec. 1. Jowett, ii, 524.   6. Lewes, 1, 10 11.
7. Grote's Plato, iii, 248.   8. Works, ch. xliv, p. 4.
9. Grote's Plato, iii, 247, 248, 249.

God (神) for the power of Motion and also of *vis inertiæ* which he possesses. In the formed Kosmos this Fate or First God is inherent in the divided Primordial Air which is Mind or *Shang-te*; but, with regard to origin He generated that Air or Mind or *Shang-te*.

(33.) By the "Great Extreme" in this paragraph is meant the self-existent Fate or God; although, properly, He does not receive that designation until the formation of the Kosmos displays His power; or, when the Matter in which He is inherent divides into two kinds in order to generate the world.

(34.) The animated Kosmos is properly speaking "The Great Extreme, which grows up from Chaos, and forms one whole, just like a tree with its numberless branches. When the end of each Kalpa arrives, then generation ceases for a while, and all things return to the bosom of Chaos or The Great Extreme, *i. e.* Fate or God inherent in the Primordial Air.

(35.) The revolutions of the Seasons, as well as the greater revolutions of the Kosmos, are all brought about by the power of the inherent Unity or God (神), who adorns all nature by His presence.[1]

(36—42.) The Light and Darkness are the twofold division of the Primordial Air or "Mind," when the latter comes forth from Chaos to generate the world, his body. The inherent self-existent Fate or God must not be confounded with this twofold animated Air. The latter is properly speaking "The Great Extreme" while the proper title of the former is "The Infinite"; and the inseparability of the two is expressed by the conjunction "and," thus, "Infinite *and* Great Extreme." These must never be separated or confounded together. Before Chow-tze adopted this phrase to describe the Great Origin of all things, there was danger, according to Choo-tze, of the Incorporeal Fate or God being confounded with the Primordial Air in which He is inherent, and which He animates by His presence, both being included under the one title "Great Extreme," just as they are under the one title "Nature." In par. 42. "The Great Extreme" refers to Fate or God, who, as the Divine Reason, makes Mind to be Mind, yet Reason and Mind must not be confounded together. They are totally distinct although not separate things.

(43.) In the Yih King the formation of the Kosmos is expressed in numbers. One or "The Great Monad" which is Mind, or *Shang-te*, or Heaven, is the Light or subtile Ether; Two or Duality is Darkness or the grosser Air or Matter (Earth); and the union of these two, forms the Triad, which is the Kosmos and also The First Man. These are the "Three Powers of Nature." The Monad consists of Unity inherent in One; the latter being generated by the former; but it is unnecessary always to state this, and hence The Great Monad is styled "The Great Extreme," although in reality he receives this title merely in virtue of the inherent Unity, or Reason, or Fate or God (神).

Pythagoras held that Monad "is the fountain of all number. The Duad is imperfect and passive, and the cause of increase and division. The Triad, composed of the Monad and Duad, partakes of the nature of both,"[2] &c.

(44.) "The Great Extreme" in this paragraph is the Primordial Air or Great Monad or *Shang-te*, who by his gyrations generates Light and Darkness under the

---

1. Yih King, bk. iv, ch. vi, (first par.).   2. Enf. 1, 384.

guidance of the inherent Unity or God (神). In paragraph 45, the latter or "Incorporeal Great Extreme" is meant.

(46.) The meaning of the title 易經 is "The Classic of Change;" that is to say, the Yih King is the Classic which contains the history of the various Changes and Transmutations which take place during the formation of the various parts of the Kosmos. As however Fate or Unity or the First God (神) never changes, it is the Primordial Air or The Great Monad or *Shang-te*, in which He is inherent, which undergoes these various changes, and hence this Air is designated "change." The sentence in the Yih King, therefore, to which Choo-tsze alludes, means that "change has the Great Extreme, which generated the Two E," &c. That is to say, in the centre of The Great Monad or the Primordial Air, which divides into the Two E, Light and Darkness, is the First God (神), who is inherent in it and who confers upon it the power to act as the Demiurge in the generation of the Kosmos. The Two E or Khāen-khwăn, as this twofold Air is designated in the Yih King, form The Great Extreme, properly so called, who generates the Kosmos from his own substance, Air, and who rules and governs it when generated. "(The Great Extreme) is Khāen-khwăn united in one (Air). Because of his *one* God (神) he is called The Great Extreme." "Khāen-khwăn is The Ruler (*Shang-te*) who governs the Myriad of things, and pervades the midst of the Six Children; but God (神) refers to Him who adorns the Myriad of things."[1]

Choo-tsze and the other Confucianists, therefore, most distinctly insist that the one Indivisible Unity or God (神) is far above *Shang-te* or the animated Kosmos, upon whom "He rides as a man rides upon a horse;" and this animated Kosmos, like Plato's, is only the second God, or the Demon-god body and soul. It is plain also that Mind, or Light, or *Shang-te*, (like the elder Cupid or Light) is the first generated god, born from chaos.

(47—50.) God inherent in the Primordial Air, is the Great Origin of all things. God (神) is the Incorporeal Reason, and the Air is the corporeal Receptacle. When the subtile Air or Mind is in chaos, that is His Rest or non-manifestation; and when all things spring forth into being, that is His Motion or manifestation. The title "Great Extreme" given to Mind or *Shang-te* corresponds exactly to the title "Tigillum" given to Jupiter, which signifies "the centre beam of a house."

---

1. Yih King, bk. iv, ch. vi, imp. ed. (vol. xlv, 17, 15). Com.

HEAVEN AND EARTH.

This section opens with the formation of the Kosmos from the Great Origin of all things, viz., God (神) inherent in the Primordial Air. This animated Primordial Air, which is The Great Monad or Heaven or *Shang-te*, now begins to revolve, the power of Motion being bestowed upon him by the inherent First God (神). At first the entire circle is dark, watery, and chaotic, but as the whole mass revolves, Light or the ethereal Fire is set free, and ascends up to the highest and outermost circle of the heavens, shining through the Air and constituting the animated visible Heaven; the lower portion forming his ethereal vehicle. The sediment which floats about in this muddy watery chaos, settles down, in consequence of Heaven's gyrations, and congealing, forms the Earth which remains immoveable in the centre, resting as Anaximenes held, "like a broad leaf" on the Air of Heaven. The Sun, Moon and Stars are made from the Primordial Air and are therefore animated, like all the other parts of the Kosmos, by the one God (神) inherent in it, and in all its parts; who pervades all things without division of substance.

(Par. 1–4.) The first agreement with western Philosophy to be noticed here is, that during the Chaotic period, the whole face of Nature is enveloped in Darkness.[1] Such was the doctrine of the Egyptians, for instance, who are said to have deified the *mus araneus*, which is blind, because they considered that "darkness was older than light."[2] This darkness is the Female Principle of the Confucianists, and is designated *Yin*; which is the *Yoni* of the Hindoos, and the *Juno* of the Greeks and Romans. According to the Confucianist Cosmogony, therefore, Darkness or Night is the Mother of the Gods. This was also the doctrine of Orpheus and others.[3]

The firstborn form Chaos and Night, is the Light, (see par. 6). This Light is a pure ethereal Fire and is made to be an intellectual Mind, as we have seen, by the inherent Divine Reason or God. "Intellect, Sensation and Motion belong to the Light; bodily form to the Darkness."[4] This Light, or ethereal Intellectual Fire, or Mind, is situated at the highest and outermost circle of Heaven, "the highest part of the upper portion" of which "is most pure and bright." (par. 8.) "Mind is the brilliant portion of the Air."[5] That is to say, he is the highest of the nine spiral circles of which the animated Heaven consists. This animated Heaven by his gyrations preserves the Earth in existence, and carries around with him Day and Night and the Sun, Moon and Stars. This Light or Mind is designated *Khëen* in the Yih King; "Khëen is the commencement of all things, hence he is designated Heaven, and Light, and Father, and Prince."[6] Lastly, this Mind or Heaven being now born from Chaos consorts with Earth, his Mother, and these two generate all things; "*Khëen* is Heaven, and hence he is styled Father; *Khwăn* is Earth, and hence she is styled Mother." "Heaven and Earth are the Father and Mother of all things." "Mar-

---

1. See plate ii. fig. 1.   2. Cud. 1, 399.
3. Ibid, 398.   4. Choo-tsze's Works, ch. ii, p. 19.
5. Ibid, ch. xliv, p. 2.   6. Bk. i, ch. i, Com. bk. iv, (說卦傳) ch. xi.

riage is the great principle of Heaven and Earth. If Heaven and Earth had not conjugal intercourse with each other, the myriad of things could not exist. Marriage is the beginning and end of mankind."[1] In every one of these particulars Mind or *Shang-te* is the identical Jupiter of the West: for. 1. Jupiter is the Light, the first born from Darkness and Chaos; e. gr. "But the earth being then invisible by reason of the darkness, a light breaking out through the ether illumined the whole creation; this light being said by him (Orpheus) to be that highest of all Beings (before mentioned) which is called also counsel and life."[2] 2 Jupiter is an ethereal Fire. "The Stoics held that the ether was signified by the name of Jove."[3] "Let Jupiter, therefore, be no longer that fiery and ethereal substance, which the ancient Pagans, according to Plutarch, supposed him to be," &c. 3 Jupiter was designated "Mind"; e. gr. "By Zeus the Greeks understood that Mind of the world which framed all things in it, and containeth the whole world."[4] 4 Jupiter is the highest of Heaven's nine spheres; "All things," says Cicero, "are connected together in nine spheres, of which one is the celestial and outermost, which comprehends and encompasses all the rest, the Supreme God himself confining and containing the others." "But here" remarks Dr. Mosheim, "Cicero's *summus Deus* is the last of those nine spheres of which the ancients supposed Heaven to consist,"[5] 5 Heaven or Jupiter preserves the world in being by his gyrations; hence he is thus invoked in a passage in Euripides, "Thee, the self-sprung, I invoke, who enfoldest the whole nature of things, whirling in ethereal gyration, around whom day and variegated night, and the countless throng of stars perpetually dance."[6] And, lastly; Jupiter and his Mother Earth are the Great Father and Mother of all things; "Earth first produced Heaven radiant with constellations; that is, the fiery and more subtile particles of matter flew off from the rest, and rose to loftier regions, forming the heavens and the stars, &c. Then Earth consorting with her own offspring Heaven, gave birth to several Deities, and last of all to Saturn,"[7] &c.

The Confucian chief god *Shang-te*, then, is Mind, or Light, an active, intelligent Principle, inherent in Chaos, from which he forms his body the visible world, and rules and governs it as the Mind does the body in Man. So also; "Chaos which was also called Night, was in the most ancient times worshipped as one of the superior divinities." Besides the material Principle, "the Egytians admitted an active principle, or intelligent power, eternally united with the chaotic mass, by whose energy the elements were separated and bodies were formed, and who continually presides over the universe, and is the efficient cause of all things."[8]

This Mind or Light or *Shang-te* is only the second hypostasis, being the Demiurge or second god, who owes his existence and all his powers to the Eternal Fate or Incorporeal Reason, or First god; so also the Egyptians, "acknowledge before the heaven and in the heaven a living power, and place pure mind above the world as the Demiurgus and architect thereof."[9] This maker of the world "was not the supreme Being, but......far below the parent and founder of all things."[10] "Among the rulers," of the world, "Jamblicus assigns the first place to the Demiurgic Mind, which he tells us is Ammon, Phtha, and Osiris."[11] With these gods therefore, *Shang-te* ranks.

---

1. Yih King, bk. ii, Diag. 54, bk. iv, (說卦) ch. x.   2. Cud. i, 503.
3. Ibid, p. 428, note.   4. Ibid, p. 424.   5. Ibid, ii, 127, note.
6. Cud. i, 631 note.   7. Ibid, p. 406. note.   8. Enf. i, 99.
9. Cud. i, 540.   10. Ibid, p. 598, note.   11. Ibid, p. 662, note.

Thus although one God (神) κατ' εξοχην, called Fate, Reason, Nature, &c., who is in reality the Father of all things, is plainly acknowledged by the Confucianists, yet this First God is wholly neglected by them; and the *second* God, or *Shang-te*, receives all the worship due in reality to the First; no higher God being recognised in the state religion than this Demiurge, who is regarded as the Creator himself. In this however the Confucianists are not singular; *e. gr.* "The Father perfected all things, that is the intelligible ideas (for these are those things which are complete and perfect) and delivered them to the second God to rule over them. Wherefore, whatsoever is produced by this God according to its own exemplar and the intelligible essence, must needs owe its original also to the highest Father. Which *second* God the generations of men *commonly take for the first*, they looking up no higher than to the immediate architect of the world."[1] The First God, to whom *Shang-te* and all the other gods are subject, is designated "Fate" by the Confucianists, and He was so designated by some of the western philosophers also; *e. gr.* some pagan philosophers "though they verbally acknowledged a deity yet supposed a certain fate superior to it, and not only to all their other petty gods, but also *to Jupiter himself*."[2] And as Choo-tsze designates this Fate " God " (神) so do the Stoics call Him " God " (Θεος, Deus); "you mention Nature, Fate, Fortune, names of this kind are all *names of God* variously employing his power."[3] Choo-tsze "Being asked the difference between Heaven and Providence, Nature and Fate; and whether 'Heaven' refers to spontaneous existence; 'Providence' to flowing forth and being conferred upon all things; 'Nature' to the entire body (*i. e.* God and Primordial Air together) which the myriad of things obtain in order to exist; and 'Fate' to each matter and thing having its own law; yet, spoken of unitedly, then Heaven, Fate, Providence, and Nature, all designate the same (Being); is this correct? He replied: Just so. Some persons, however, now assert that the title 'Heaven' does not mean the azure sky; yet, in my opinion, the azure sky *must not be omitted.*"[4] Thus in the complete Heaven or Kosmos we have three things united to form one being or god, viz., 1. The visible Heaven (the body) 2. the subtile ether or Mind (the Rational Soul), and 3. Fate, the First God whose Hegemonikon is "Mind." These three united form the complete God "Heaven" or *Shang-te*, and hence there is no such thing as a personal God, distinct and separate from matter, to be found in the Confucian Classics.[5] *Shang-te* or Mind is the soul which wraps the world round, or contains it, and who governs it as the soul governs the body in Man. Such is the doctrine of the Western Philosophers; "As we are governed by a soul, so also the world has a soul which contains it, and this soul is called Ζεὺς or Jupiter."[6]

(5, 6.) The following Circle used by the Chinese Philosophers to illustrate the doctrine of the endless succession of similar worlds, will assist the student to understand that theory:

1. Cud. i, 484.
2. Ibid, p. 7.
3. Ibid, p. 249 note.
4. Works, ch. xlii, p. 1.
5. See below par. 29.
6. Cud. ii, 296, note.

NOTE. 147

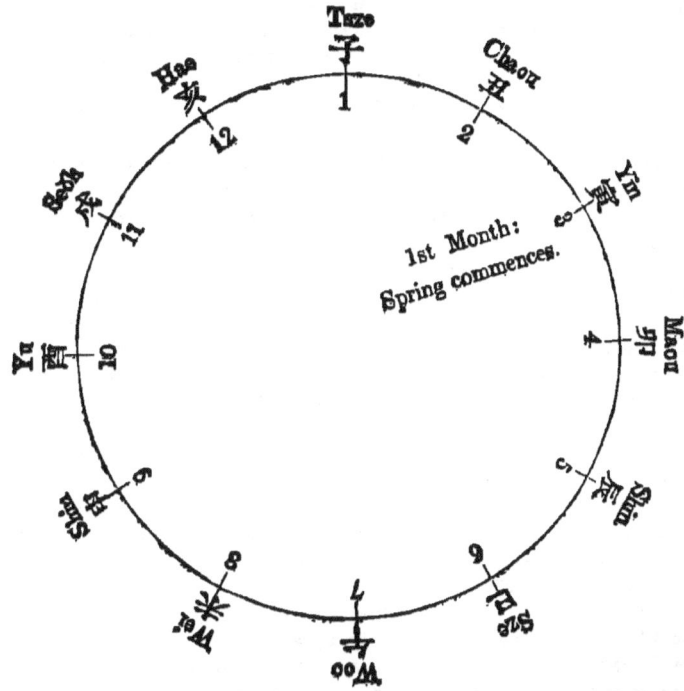

Each complete revolution of this circle is called a Yuen or Kalpa, (元) and consists of 129,600 years. Each subdivision is called a Hwuy (會), and is supposed to consist of 10,800 years. In the first Hwuy (*Tsze*) Heaven or *Shang-te* comes forth, the door of the *Ovum Mundi* being opened, in which he was preserved from the preceding Deluge. In the second (*Chaou*) his wife Earth comes out; and in the third (*Yin*) the First Man appears, who is their son, or the union of both his parents (Monad and Dnad or Heaven and Earth) in human form. This Man comes forth from the *Ovum Mundi* in Spring, and Confucius made this period the first month of the year, in imitation of the Hea Dynasty.[1] This First Man is evidently the Kosmos or *Shang-te* in human form, while the Kosmos or *Shang-te* or Mind is merely this First Man in his deified or Mundane character; and hence we are distinctly told in the Confucian Classics that "MAN is *the Mind* of Heaven and Earth."[2]

The Deluge which reduces all things to primitive Chaos, prevails during the last or 12th Hwuy, which is the ninth period from the appearance of the First Man, as the period of the Noetic Deluge was; and, on the return to the first Hwuy (*Tsze*) the Kosmos is again generated from Chaos as before. The Cycle of 60, formed by the combination of the above circle with another of 10 divisions, is said to have been invent-

---

1. Lun Yu, bk. xv, ch. x.
2. Le Ke, sec. iv, (禮運) p. 56.

ed by "Naou (Noah?) the Great" after the Deluge.[1] The period of the destruction of the Universe is represented under the Pŏ Diagram of the Yĭh King, in which each round of Nature terminates, and all things come to an end in consequence of the universal depravity of mankind.[2] The "Mean Man" gains the ascendency in this Diagram, and the "Prince" or Model Man or *Shang-te* retires into quiescence. At the following or Fŭh Diagram however, this Prince, or Heaven, or *Shang-te*, the "Mind of Heaven and Earth," who is preserved in the *Ovum Mundi* from destruction, by the inherent Fate or First God (神), arouses himself from his "non-manifestation," as Choo-tsze terms it, and precedes to generate a new body or Kosmos from the Primordial Air, or Matter of the old world.

In the Yĭh King each "spreading out" of the world is attributed to Khëen or animated Heaven, and is compared to the opening of a door, through which all creation issues forth; and each return to Chaos or the *Ovum Mundi*, or "The Great Receptacle" as it is called, is attributed to Khwăn or animated Earth, and is compared to the shutting of a door, so that all things may be safely stored up until the period arrives for them to issue forth again after the Deluge has subsided; "Hence shutting the door refers to Khwăn, and opening the door to Khëen. Each shutting and opening is Change (i. e. a revolution of the world); and the everlasting succession (of these revolutions) is pervading without obstruction."[3] These are called the "Great Revolutions," and they are compared to a year; e. gr. "A day has a day's revolution; a month has a month's revolution; and a year has a year's revolution. Heaven and Earth's commencements and terminations are the Great Revolutions." "Shaou Pih-wan says that each complete Great Revolution resembles a year."[4]

"After an interval," says Seneca, "in which the deity (i. e. Jupiter, the Mind or soul of Chaos) will be intent upon his own conceptions, the world will be entirely renewed, every animal will be reproduced, and a race of men free from guilt, and born under happier stars, will repeople the earth. Degeneracy and corruption will, however, again creep into the world; for, it is only when the human race is young, that innocence remains upon the earth. The grand course of things from the birth to the destruction of the world, which according to the Stoics, is to be repeated with endless succession, is accomplished within a certain period. This period or fated round of nature, is probably what the ancients meant by the Great Year."[5]

"The Cosmogony of an anonymous Etrurian preserved by Suidas......limits the duration of the universe to a period of 12,000 years, 600 of which passed in the production of the visible world, before the formation of man. Another doctrine ascribed to the Etrurians, which agrees with the tenets of the Stoics, is, the entire renovation of nature after a long period or *great year*, when a similar succession of events would again commence."[6]

Plato also held that "the world will remain for ever, but that by the action of its animating principle, it accomplishes certain periods within which every thing returns to its ancient place and state. This periodical revolution of nature is called the Platonic or Great Year."[7]

---

1. 綱鑑, Vol. i, p. 24.
2. Compare Genesis, ch. vi, 5.
3. Bk. III, (上) ch. xl.
4. 性理, &c. sec. viii, p. 13.
5. Enf. i, 841.
6. Enf. i, 111.
7. Ibid, p. 238. Jowett, Vol. iv, p. 198.

Xenophanes thought that the Earth "had at one time been covered with water, in proof of which he noticed the numerous shells found inland and on mountain tops, together with the prints of various fish which he had observed in the quarries of Syracuse, in the island of Paros and elsewhere. From these facts he inferred that the earth had once been covered with water, and even that it would again be so covered at some future time to the destruction of animal and human life."[1] Herodotus from the same premises, draws a like inference with regard to lower Egypt.[2]

With regard to the formation of the First Man, Plato held that he was made from the four Elements Fire, Air, Water and Earth.[3]

"It was, we know, the belief of *nearly every nation*, that the Earth impregnated by the power of the ether and the stars, brought forth from its womb in different places, the progenitors of the human family. Hence Brutus commanded by the oracle to salute his mother, kissed the earth, an action of his that very few have rightly comprehended. Similar was the notion of the Gauls, when they affirmed that they were the descendants of Dis, that is, the Earth."[4]

(7, 8, 9, 10.) Heaven and Earth having come forth from the *Ovum Mundi*, in which they were preserved during the Deluge, now become the Great Father and Mother of all things, and with these form one complete whole which is worshipped entire and in all its parts and members, in detail, in the state religion of China.[5] Heaven or *Shang-te* surrounds the Earth, and Earth itself is made from his substance, so that the whole Kosmos is styled "Heaven." Thus *Shang-te* is the Heaven above the Earth, and also the portion below the Earth, that is to say, Hades. He is, in a word, a Great Monad and yet all things; Earth, Sun, Moon, and Stars, Mountains, Rivers, Trees, Plants, Birds, Beasts, Reptiles &c., being all made from his substance, Air; and all being his various parts and members. Hence all are worshipped equally with himself. "With regard to the whole (Heaven or Kosmos), then Earth is this one Heaven, and the six children are also this one Heaven," or *Shang-te*.[6] The family saved from each Deluge, according to the Yih King, are Khëen, Mind or *Shang-te* or Heaven, Khwän or Earth, his wife, three sons and their three wives (and sisters). This family of Eight are the *Dii Majorum Gentium* of the Pagan world.[7]

So also in the West, the animated Kosmos or Jupiter was called Heaven; e. gr. "The world, and that which by another name is called Heaven (cœlum), by whose circumgyrations all things are governed, ought to be believed a Numen, eternal, immense, such as never was made, and shall never be destroyed."[8] "Let the universe then be called Heaven, or by any other name which it usually receives,"[9] &c. Hence this Heaven or Jupiter is called by Valerius Soranus "*Deus unus at omnes.*" And Jupiter himself addresses the other gods as "Cœlicolœ, mea membra, Dei."[10] &c. The portion below the Earth, or Hades, was also Heaven or Jupiter; and hence Orpheus calls "Jupiter and Hades (personified, Pluto), one and the same God."[11] Aristotle states that Anaximenes also regarded his Primordial Air as "God," that is to say, as Heaven or Jupiter.[12]

(11, 12.) The Primordial Air or Great Monad (大一) generates the visible

---

1. Grote's Plato, i, 19. 2. Herodotus, ii, 12. (Rawlinson).
3. Grote's Plato, iii, 277. Jowett, iii, 175. 4. Cud. 1, 402 note. 5. Chin. Rep. iii, 50.
6. Yih King, bk. iii, ch.xi, Kang-he. (Imp. Ed) 7. Ibid, bk. iv, ch. x.
8. Cud. i, 210. 9. Timæus, sec. i. 10. Cud, ii, 206, 227.
11. Ibid. p. 222. 12. Ibid. i, 161, 186.

world from his own substance. The subtile portion or Ether is his Mind, and the grosser Air he forms into the visible world as his body, which he pervades and animates, as the Mind pervades and animates the body in Man. Outside the whole body of Heaven or the Kosmos, is a hard ethereal shell which preserves this divine animal from destruction : so that, even in its arranged state the Kosmos is regarded as an egg, in which every thing living is preserved, and which floats on the Chaotic waters with its eight inhabitants while the Deluge prevails.

(15.) Heaven or *Shang-te*'s natural colour is a deep azure approaching to black.[1] Both Hindoos and Egyptians represent this Great Father "Heaven," as being of a black or dark azure colour. The latter called this Demiurgus Cneph, and worshipped him, personified, "in a statue of human form, and a blackish sky-coloured complexion ...... and thrusting forth an egg out of his mouth, by which was meant the world."[2]

(19, 20, 21.) Mind, or the subtile ether (*Shang-te*), is endowed with intelligence by Fate, and holds a middle place, as we have seen, between this First God and the grosser Primordial Air which he (*Shang-te*) pervades and animates, and from which he forms his body Heaven and Earth or the visible world. Compared with the First God he is regarded as being "corporeal," while, in comparison with his body the world, he is considered to be a "spiritual" substance. The distinction between this Mind or the second god, and Fate or the First God, is insisted upon most distinctly in par. 20. Mind or *Shang-te*, would cease to be a Mind, if Fate or the First God (the Incorporeal Reason) were not inherent in it; so that, these two, although wholly different and distinct as to nature, must never be regarded as separated from each other. *Shang-te* or Mind, the Intellectual Ethereal Fire, is the Ruler of all the lesser Gods, as well as of the world his body ; and if Heaven or the Kosmos were not animated by this ethereal Mind, then, "Oxen would produce horses, and peach trees would send forth plum-blossoms," there being no Ruler to generate the various parts of the universe according to their kind. In Chaos this Demiurgic Mind or *Shang-te* remains quiescent and passive, as it were engaged in meditation, until the period arrives for the arrangement of a new Kosmos from the ruins of the old world ; that is to say, from the Primordial Matter in which Le is inherent, and of which he is the most subtile and ethereal portion. This Mind is designated "Kheen" in the Yih King because he is "Hard" ether, and he is called "*Shang-te*" because he rules his body the world, just as the Mind rules the body in Man. The complete Kosmos or Heaven, therefore, is merely a Man, while Man is a Microcosm.[3] "Heaven (*Shang-te* or the Kosmos) is a Mould—a Great Man ; Man is a little Heaven" (Microcosm). "Especially must this be done by us, whose ancestor (Confucius) and Heaven (*Shang-te* or the Kosmos) are one."[4] "The Sage is the Active Principle (用 ; i. e. Soul) of Heaven and Earth."[5] "Man's head is round like Heaven, and his feet are square like Earth."[6] According to the Yih King Heaven or *Shang-te* or the Kosmos is but a Man. Plato also held that "the cranium (in Man) was made spherical in exterior form like the Kosmos," i. e. "Heaven" or Jupiter.[7]

(22, 23.) The period during which Mind or *Shang-te* is quiescent, is, when he is shut up in the *Ovum Mundi*, to preserve him during the period of the Deluge. From

---

1. Yih King, bk. 1, p. 13. 2. Cud. 1, 598. 3. See also next par.
4. Chin. Rep. xviii, 254. 5. 性理, &c. sec. xxxviii, p. 7.
6. Choo-tsze's Works, ch. xlii, p. 31. 7. Grote's Plato, iii, 264. Jowett, ii, 538.

this he comes forth to generate all things. This Khëen or Mind is the second god and pervades all things, being in fact the rational soul of the world. He is the Mind in Man, as well as the principle of life in the lower creation. That which pervaded the το παν in the West was called Θεος or Deus, Νους or Mens, and was the second god, and this same thing precisely, the Confucianists call the 神 or God *Shang-te* or Mind; the second God. Thus the soul of the Kosmos is called "Mind" both in the Confucian and in the Western systems of Philosophy; in both also, he is the subtile ether or the Light, endowed with reason by the First God, or the Incorporeal Fate, to which latter, in both, precisely the same titles are given, and the same attributes ascribed. The parallel, both as to the First God and also as to the second, is beyond question. Of Jupiter, the rational soul of the Kosmos, Virgil says:

"Mens agitat molem, et magno se corpore miscet.
Inde hominum pecudumque genua, vitæque volantum,
Et quæ marmoreo fert monstra sub æquore pontus." &c.1

Aristotle held "that animals have souls derived from that most subtile ether or soul which pervades Heaven, the Air, and the Stars."2 "Chrysippus asserted the ether to be the principal god, and to pervade all things." "Souls are thus bound to and connected with God as being parts of and deceptions from himself."3 Plato held that the soul in Man "is derived by emanation from God; but that this emanation was not immediate, but *through the intervention of the soul of the world*, which was itself debased by some material admixture," &c. (*i. e.* with the *Anima*; the *Khwän* of the Yĭh King).4 "Man, according to the Stoics, is an image of the world; one whole composed of body and Mind. The Mind of Man is a spark of that Divine fire which is the soul of the world."5 Pythagoras, Empedocles, and the philosophers of the Italic school, held that "we men have not only a conjunction amongst ourselves with one another, but also with the gods above us, and with brute animals below us; because there is but one spirit, which, like a soul, pervades the whole world, and unites all the parts thereof together."6 Hence as Heaven, Earth and all things are *Shang-te* in China, so were they Jupiter in the West. This explains the statement of Mencius, that, "That whereby man differs from the lower animals is but small."7

This Mind or *Shang-te*, the animated Air, is generated by the First God, who is called Fate, and "The Good" (see Part I, above, par. 2, 7). So also Jupiter. Plato, for instance, held that this "Mind or Intellect" was generated by the first "Hypostasis," τ'αγαθον,8 and this Mind henceforth usurps the place, titles, and attributes of the First God, and is "generally by all men looked upon as the first and highest God."9 So it is in China; although the Confucianists distinctly acknowledge an eternal, self-existent Unity or Divine Reason higher than Mind or *Shang-te*, who is but the second god and the Demiurgus, yet, all worship this second god, as being "the immediate architect of the world," and virtually exclude the first God altogether.10

(27, 28.) Hence, while Choo-tsze holds that there must be a Ruler in the Kosmos, he denies, like all the rest of the pagan world, that this Ruler is a personal being separate from Matter. He is merely a Mind or soul who acts under a higher power, Fate, who "rides upon him as a man rides upon a horse."

1. Æneid, lib. vi, ver, 724–732. 2. Cud. II, 240, note.
3. Ibid, p. 290, note; 98, note. 4. Enf. I, 238. 5. Ibid, p. 342.
6. Cud. II, 240. 7. Legge's Mencius, p. 201.
8. Cud. II, 368. 9. Ibid, p. 385, note. 10. See below, par. 27.

(29, 30, 31.) Thus, on the authority of the Confucian Classics, Heaven or the Kosmos consists of three things united in one whole, viz, 1°. The Eternal Fate or First God (至神), 2° Mind or *Shang-te*, the Intellectual Ether, the second god, and the Demiurgus; and 3° The visible Heaven or Kosmos which is his body. These are never separated, but form one whole animated Kosmos, in the centre of which the Earth is placed, which is upheld by the swift gyrations of this Heaven or *Shang-te*.

(35, 36.) The twofold division of the Primordial Air in generating each species is into a Male and a Female. To generate Man it divides into an *Animus* and *Anima Mundi*, who are the Great Father and Mother of all things. The Light, which is "Father," and "Prince," and "Ruler," is the Masculine Principle, and the Darkness which is styled "Mother," is the Female Principle. These each generate a body; the former generates Heaven and the latter Earth, and these two, body and soul, are the Great Father and Mother when regarded as *two*, while, regarded as *one* they constitute the Great Hermaphroditic deity Heaven or *Shang-te*, the Great Monad who generates all things from and within himself, and who is thus the Hermaphroditic "Heaven" or Jupiter of the Western philosophers. "When they assume form," says Choo-tsze, "*Khēen* (the Light) becomes Heaven, and *Khwăn* (the Darkness) becomes Earth."¹ He also said "the expressions 'the generating of Heaven,' 'the generating of Earth;' 'the completing the Demon (*Khwăn*),' 'the completing the Ruler (*Khēen*),' means the same as this, 'The Great Extreme (the Air) moving and resting generated the Earth and the Heaven'" (*Yin* and *Yang* complete).² The statement of Woo Lin-chuen has been already quoted, that "Khēen-khwăn is the Ruler (帝, *i. e. Shang-te*) who governs the myriad of things, and pervades the midst of the six children." *Shang-te* then, like Jupiter, is the twofold soul of the Kosmos, and the visible world is his body which he governs as the Mind governs the body in Man. He is the "Virtuous Nature" which Man receives from this animated Heaven or Kosmos, at his birth.

(37—43.) The passage commented upon in the 37th paragraph will be found in the text of the Yih King.³ This Great Father "Heaven" and his wife "Earth" are the two great Patrons of generation, and hence they are always worshipped at marriages. "The first copy (of the marriage contract) we shall take and burn before Heaven and Earth.......(The contract) being solemnly sworn to, they knelt in humble worship before Heaven and Earth."⁴

"Confucius says, *Khēen* and *Khwăn*, (Heaven and Earth,) are the door of Change (*i. e.* of generation). *Khēen* is the 陽物 male organ of generation, and *Khwăn* is the 陰物 female organ of generation."⁵ Thus Heaven or *Shang-te* is evidently the Priapus of the west, and the Baal-peor of Scripture whose worship was "*Aperire. hymenem virgineum.*"

On this universal pagan doctrine, Arnobius (lib. 3. adv. Gentes) thus comments: "What say you, ye holy and unpolluted champions of religions? Have the gods then sexes, and do they carry about with them the impurities of genital members?...... O pure, O holy, O spotless divinities!" &c.⁶

---

1. Works, sec. xxviii, p. 1.
2. Choo-tsze; (Pandects); bk 1, p. 74. (Legge's "Notions," &c).
3. Sec. iii, ch. vi, (上). Phallic worship.   4. 王嬌鸞 &c.
5. Yih King, book iii, ch, vi. (下).   6. Cud. vol. 1, p. 507 note.

LIGHT AND DARKNESS.—THE FIVE ELEMENTS.—THE SEASONS.

We now come to the particular consideration of the twofold soul of Heaven or the animated Kosmos, viz. Light and Darkness. The Light is a subtile, intellectual Fire, or ethereal Mind, and is the rational portion of the soul; and the Darkness is the sentient or irrational portion, or the *anima mundi*. These two souls are precisely the same in the Kosmos and in Man, and hence the former is styled a Great Man, and the latter a microcosm, or "little Heaven" (*Shang-te*). In the Kosmos, the body in which these souls are inherent is the visible Heaven and Earth, Heaven being the Head, Earth the Feet, the Sun and Moon the eyes &c., and this whole animated Kosmos, body and soul (or 體 and 用) is the complete Heaven or *Shang-te* of the Confucian Classics—the chief Demon-god of the material system taught by the great Sage of China.

"Heaven belongs to the Light and is God; Earth belongs to the Darkness and is Demon."[1]

And these are so designated from their souls; *e. gr.* "The soul of the *Yang* (Heaven) is god; and the soul of the *Yin* (Earth) is Demon."[2] Hence also, Heaven and Earth are designated Light (*Yang*) and Darkness (*Yin*) respectively, Heaven being the complete Light, body and soul, and Earth being the complete Darkness, body and soul. As "*one*" these are the great Hermaphroditic Heaven or *Shang-te* body and soul, and as "*two*" they are Husband and Wife, the Great Father and Mother of all things.

(Par. 1-6, 9.) The Light and the Darkness are, in fact, two Genera, under one or other of which every portion of the whole Universe is classed; hence, Heaven belongs to the Light, Earth to the Darkness; Before belongs to the Light, Behind to the Darkness; the Left belongs to the Light, and hence it is the place of honour in China, while the Right belongs to the Darkness.[3] Every Male also, whether of Man, or Beast, or Bird, or Reptile, or Insect, belongs to the Light, and every Female to the Darkness. Also, each thing which belongs to the Light, has also in it a certain proportion of the Darkness, and *vice versâ*. Hence, as the Light is Masculine and the Darkness Feminine, every male is also female, and every female is also male[4]. The Chinese say that it is in consequence of this law that the human male can beget daughters, and the female can give birth to sons. This theory of Light and Darkness also enters extensively into the social life of the Chinese; *e. gr.* in receiving guests the Confucian rule, as laid down in the Seaou Hëŏ, is as follows; "Whoever enters with his guests yields precedence to them at every door; when they reach the innermost one, he begs leave to go in and arrange the seats, and then returns to receive the guests; and after they have repeatedly declined, he bows to them and enters. He passes through the right (*i. e.* Darkness) door, they through the left (Light). He ascends the eastern (Light), they the western (Darkness) steps. If a guest be of a lower grade, he must

---

1. 性理 &c. Sec. xxviii, p. 4.
2. Choo-tsze's Works, ch. li, p. 6.
3. See below, par. 18. 20.
4. Below, par, 17. Yih King, lii, iv, (下).

approach the steps of the host, while the latter must repeatedly decline the attention; then the guest may return to the western steps; he ascending, both host and guest must mutually yield precedence: then the host must ascend first and the guests follow. From step to step they must bring their feet togther, gradually ascending,—those on the east (Light) moving the right (Darkness) foot first, those on the west (Darkness), the left" (Light).[1] Hence, also, when a man is dying, his female relatives are sent out of the room as they belong to the Darkness, which is death; and his male relatives and friends, who belong to the Light, which is life, are introduced in order to keep him alive as long as possible. "Day and Night, *that is to say* Light and Darkness, *Death* and *Life*, Demon and God."[2]

(11, 12.) These paragraphs refer to the statement in the Yih King, "That which is Incomprehensible in the Light and the Darkness is God (神)."[3] God, who is designated by the Confucianists Fate, Reason, &c., is inherent in the Eternal Primordial Air, and with it forms one whole, as the body and soul in Man. This Primordial Air divides into two kinds, viz., Light and Darkness; and, as the Divine Unity or God which is inherent in it pervades both divisions of this Air whole and entire, and without division of substance, being a perfect Unity, He is declared to be "Incomprehensible." The Primordial Air thus dividing into a Male and a Female, generates all things. Thus the Great Origin of all things is "One yet Two, Two yet One"; the "One" or Unity being "God," and the "Two" being Light and Darkness or Ether and grosser Air, the Great Father and Mother of all things, and the Jupiter and Juno of Western Philosophy. The Kosmos composed of these "Two" is the Great Hermaphroditic Monad *Shang-te*, (太一) whose animating Principle is the Divine Unity, "The Infinite" or the απειρον of the Pagan World.

(13.) The Darkness or Female Principle, which ultimately becomes the Earth, collects and stores up within her the Air or seed of the world which the Light or Heaven scatters, and thus she generates all things.[4]

(14, 15.) The Great Extreme is, properly speaking,[5] the twofold soul of *Shang-te* or the animated Kosmos. But this double soul who is the acting Demiurgus, derives all his powers from the Divine Reason,[6] which is the real Great Extreme, inherent in this second Great Extreme, or Air, without which latter "He would not have any thing to rest upon." Hence to avoid confusion, the designation "The Infinite" is given to the real Great Extreme,[6] and thus His complete distinctness from *Shang-te* or the second Great Extreme,[7] the twofold Air in whom He is inherent, is maintained. The Root of all things, and all souls, is God (神) or "The Infinite," and the Demiurge on whom "He rides as a Man drives a chariot" is "The Great Extreme" or *Shang-te*, the twofold soul or Mind of the visible world. The relation between these three, as has been already shown, is thus stated by Choo-tsze; "Mind,[7] compared with Nature (fig. 4) is more material; but compared with the Air,[8] he is certainly more spiritual."

The real Great Extreme or "The Infinite,"[6] while He is the Author of all motion possessed by the second Great Extreme or *Shang-te*,[7] is nevertheless Himself immoveable; and in this we have another added to the many proofs that this First God of the

---

1. "Middle Kingdom." vol. i, p. 539   2. Yih King, bk. iii, ch. v. (上). Imp. Ed.
3. Bk. iii, ch. v, (上).   4. "Heaven and Earth," per. 37.
5. Plate I. Fig. 5.   6. Plate, I, Fig. 4.
7. Ibid, Fig. 5.   8. Ibid, Fig. 6.

Confucianists is the identical First God of Western Philosophers; e. gr. the First God (Θεος) is designated by Aristotle "τὸ πρῶτον κινοῦν ἀκίνητον, the first immoveable mover."[1] Hence in the Confucian jargon this God (神) "moves yet moves not, rests yet rests not"; i. e. He confers these powers upon *Shang-te* or the animated Primordial Air in whom He is inherent, while He Himself, as He occupies "the pivot" or centre of motion, is not affected by either the Motion or the Rest.

(22.) Here again, the First god, Fate or Reason, is scrupulously distinguished from the second god, viz., the Primordial Air, or Monad, or *Shang-te*, in whom He is inherent; *Shang-te* or the Air, is His Ethereal Receptacle, and He makes this Air to be a Mind by His inherent presence.

(23, 24.) The Primordial Air is not only Light and Darkness, or the animated Heaven and Earth, but these two Beings are styled astronomically, 太陽 the Sun, and 太陰 the Moon.

(25.) In this paragraph Choo-tsze gives a full description of the divided Primordial Air or two great Principles of all things, Light and Darkness, the double soul or *Animus-anima* of the visible Heaven and Earth.[2] The Circle or Universe composed of these two, is thus represented by the Chinese, with the exception of the cardinal points which are added for the sake of clearness.

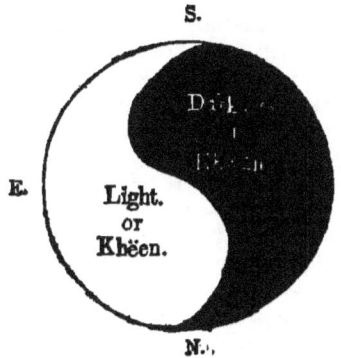

a. The Light is the Animus Mundi, or the Rational soul of the world; and the Darkness is the Anima Mundi or the sentient and Irrational soul of the world; for "The soul of the *Yang* (Heaven) is God (the Light), and the soul of the *Yin* (Earth) is Demon (the Darkness).

b. This complete circle is the Demongod *Shang-te*; for, "The Darkness is Demon, the Light is god (神)." "Demon and god, are the Air."[3]

c. These are designated, the Light *Khëen* and the Darkness *Khwăn*, in the Yih King; and the body of this double soul is the visible world or Heaven and Earth.[4] These two souls "fill up the midst of Heaven and Earth" and animate them, so that these two Beings have the power "to make and transmute," and thus become the Great Father and Mother of all things. The animated Heaven or *Shang-te*, soul and body, is the first-born from the Chaotic egg, like the Love or Cupid of western Cosmogony, and the animated Earth (Yin, Yoni, or Juno) is his wife, and these two Beings, according to the Yih King, come out with "the six Children" three sons and their three wives, constituting a family of eight deities (the Dii Majorum Gentium of the west), from the *Ovum Mundi* in which they are preserved from a fearful Deluge which utterly destroys a previous world, in consequence of the degeneracy of its inhabitants. Heaven and Earth are, in fact, the *Cœlus* and *Terra* of western Cosmogony, and are the oldest of the gods; "Heaven," says

---

1. Cud. ii, 84.
2. Plate I, fig. 5.
3. Choo-tsze's Works, ch. li, pp. 3, 6.
4. "Heaven and Earth," par. 36.

Choo-tsze, "belongs to the Light and is God (神); Earth belongs to the Darkness and is Demon (鬼)."¹

d. This Light and Darkness or the Demon-god *Shang-te,* the double soul of the Kosmos, is the subtile or more ethereal portion of the Primordial Air, and, as we have seen, is generated by the First God (神) who is designated in the Yih King "The God who adorns all things;" and Choo-tsze, as we have also seen, distinctly and carefully distinguishes this First God from the second god or *Shang-te* who is merely the chief Demon-god (鬼神). He states plainly that the Demon-god is "not the God who adorns all things" and who is the 至神 or First God of the Yih King. This latter he designates "Fate," and makes *Shang-te* subject to Him. The Light or Rational soul of the animated Kosmos is the Hægemonikón of the First God or Incorporeal Reason, and this latter makes that soul to be an Intellectual Mind by dwelling in it; "*Khèen* is the commencement of all things, and hence he is designated 'Heaven,' and 'Father,' and 'Prince.'" And Choo-tsze says, "Intellect, Sensation, and Motion belong to the Light; bodily substance to the Darkness." There can be no doubt whatever, therefore, that the *Shang-te* of the Confucian Classics is the identical Jupiter of the western Philosophers, viz., the subtile, fiery ether, endowed with intellect by Fate or the First God, and which is situated at the outermost circle of the visible Heaven, "The honourable Sovereign Mind" which is invisible to human eyes; for, "Mind is the brilliant portion of the Air." In this Mind the First God dwells and acts chiefly, for, "If there were no Mind, then Fate (God) would not have any thing to rest upon."² And this Mind is the second or Corporeal Great Extreme, the ethereal body of the First God; for, "Mind is the Great Extreme." This Mind is also, as we have seen, regarded as spiritual when compared with his body the visible Heaven and Earth. The First God, as we have also seen, is the real "Great Extreme;" but, lest he should be confounded with *Shang-te* or Mind, He is styled "The Infinite;" and to indicate the inseparable connection between the two the phrase "Infinite *and* Great Extreme" is used, which is equivalent to "Reason *and* Mind." Reason without Mind would have no means of acting, and Mind without Reason would cease to be Mind.

e. As Mind or *Shang-te* pervades all things hence the twofold soul in Man is called, the Rational portion god (神), and the Sentient portion demon (鬼). "Heaven and Earth are one thing with my body; that which is designated Demon-god (*Shang-te*) is my own Air" (*i.e.* twofold soul).³ "That which Heaven and Earth possess in common with Men is called Kwei-shin"⁴ (Demon-god or double-soul). Hence the twofold soul in Man is Mind or the Demon-god *Shang-te,* who is also the double animating Principle in Beasts, Birds, Reptiles, Trees, (hence *Shang-te* is the Sap-god of the Hellenes; see Cox's Aryan Mythology, Vol. ii, p. 118, note), &c., &c., and these souls are the gods of the Chinese Classics, in which latter, therefore, no *personal* God distinct from Matter can be found; "Because the souls of things are considered most honourable (the Sages) distinctly designated them Demon-gods (鬼神), and established them to be the patterns of the black haired people. Thus every one would fear them, and the myriads of people would obey them."⁵ It is on this ground, viz., that Man and *Shang-te,* or the animated world body and soul are identically the same, that

---

1. 性理 &c., Sec. xxviii, 4. 2. Choo-tsze's Works, ch. xliv, 2.
3. Ibid, ch. ii, 11.   4. Ibid, p. 5.   5. Le Ke, sec. viii, p. 40.

the former is exhorted to virtue ; e. gr. "Man is one thing with Heaven and Earth, why then should he demean himself?"[1] "Heaven, Earth, and the myriad of things, are one substance with my body ; when my Mind is properly adjusted, the Mind of Heaven and Earth is properly adjusted."[2] "The 神 ($\theta \varepsilon o \varsigma$—Rational soul or Mind) in Man, is the 神 of Heaven and Earth (Mind or *Shang-te*) ; so that when Man demeans himself, he demeans Heaven and Earth. Can he then venture to do so?"[3] Hence also the First God or the Divine Reason, is inherent in Man's Mind as well as in the Mind of the Kosmos, and this is what Confucius means when he says, in the passage already quoted, "My Reason (*Taou*) is the all-pervading Unity." That Reason or Fate or God is an Indivisible Unity we have already seen. Hence Mencius says that the sage "preserves the traces of God" (神神—the Divine Reason) in the Universe.

f. It is plain from what has been stated that there are three Hypostases in the animating and governing power of the Kosmos, according to the Confucian system, viz., "Fate" or "Reason" or "The good" or "God," who is an Indivisible "Unity;" 2. "Mind" or Rational soul ; and 3. "Sentient soul" or *anima*. Hence, in forming the Universe, the First God uniting Himself with the subtile ether thus places Reason in that Rational soul ; next He places that soul in body, viz. the visible Heaven and Earth, and thus completes the animated Great Extreme or Kosmos, which Choo-tsze pronounces to be a most Divine (至神) thing. Now, we have here clearly, the "three divine hypostases of the Egyptians with the Pythagoric or Platonic trinity of first, $\tau \grave{o}$ "$\varepsilon \nu$ or $\tau' \grave{a} \gamma a \theta \grave{o} \nu$, unity and goodness itself; secondly, $\nu o \nu \varsigma$, mind ; and thirdly, $\psi \nu \chi \eta$ (*i. e.* anima) soul."[4] Further, Plato describes the formation of the Kosmos thus : "In pursuance of this reasoning, placing *intellect in soul*, and *soul in body*, he (*i. e.* the First $\theta \varepsilon o \varsigma$) constructed the universe." "He generated the universe a blessed god."[5] The $N o \nu \varsigma$ or Mind of Plato was also a double soul ; "Must we not necessarily say that the soul governing and residing in all things that move, governs also Heaven (*i. e.* the universe)? Assuredly. One or more? At least more than one; nor ought we to lay down fewer than two, the one beneficent, the other working contrary things?"[6] Hence also, "Man, according to Plato bears the image of the whole world ; both the world and Man being a compound of soul and matter, and the soul of both being partly rational and partly irrational."[7] "From this we see the nature, as well as the origin and birth of that soul which governs and rules the whole universe. That mundane soul consists of two parts &c. From this soul of the world were derived, according to Plato's opinion, those souls by which our bodies are governed. What is said of it, therefore, we are to suppose as said of these also. As the soul of the world consists of two parts, one brute and irrational, the other rational and wise, so also our minds."[8] "This Ethiopian god (previously mentioned) is that twofold principle of good and evil, the worship of which *was so general* among the nations of antiquity."[9]

"Zardusht (Zoroaster) affirmed Light and Darkness, Yezdan (Oromasdes) and Ahriman, to be the two contrary principles, which were the origin of every thing subsisting in the world ; the forms of nature being produced from the combination of these principles." "Zoroaster, adopting the principle commonly held by the ancients that

1. Works of the Two Chings, Vol. i, p. 52.
2. Chung Yung, Sec. 1, p. 25.
3. 性理 &c, Sec. xii, p. 5.
4. Cud. i, p. 601: also, pp, 484–5.
5. Timæus, ch. x : xiii. Jowett, Vol. ii, 525.
6. Cud. i, 399 note. Jowett, Vol. iv, 407.
7. Cud. i, p, 348. note.
8. Ibid, p. 335 note.
9. Ibid, ii, 166, note.

from nothing, nothing can be produced, conceived light, or those spiritual substances which partake of the active nature of fire, and darkness or the impenetrable, opaque, and passive mass of matter, to be emanations from one Eternal source."[1] "This class (Zoroaster and the ancient Magi) called the better principle God, and the worse demon."[2] "......almost all the oriental nations believe the all-pervading Light to be God."[3] It is plain then, that what the Confucianists call "damon" and "神" viz., the Darkness and the Light, the other pagans call "demon" and "God" (Θεος, Deus, &c). There can be no question therefore that the Chinese term 神 means "God" and *not* "Spirit" merely. The philosopher Hwae Nan-tsze and some others amongst the Chinese designate *both* these principles God (神), but the generality (following the Yih King) designate the Light or Good principle alone god (神), and the Darkness or Evil principle Demon (鬼); so also amongst western philosophers, "Some suppose that there are two gods, as it were of contrary arts, so that one is the author of good, the other of evil things; others call him that is the better a god, but the other a demon only."[4]

This twofold Mind or *Shang-te* is also Plutarch's "Ruler," or Jupiter; "From this (evil soul or demon), and that orderly and best substance (the Rational soul) God made it prudent and regular, and imparting, as it were, intelligent form to sensitive, regular to moving, appointed it *the Ruler* of the universe."[5] And, the Confucian Demon-god or twofold soul *Shang-te* is the Being to whom the most solemn worship is offered by the Chinese Emperors at the Altars of Heaven and Earth at Peking; "Confucius said......By sacrifices to Heaven and Earth, they (the ancient Kings) served *Shang-te*."[6] And the philosopher himself explains that by "*Shang-te*" he does not mean merely an *inanimate* visible world, but the twofold soul of the *animated* world, viz. Light and Darkness or the Great Demon-god who rules all things; he says, "The sacrifices to Heaven and Earth are to show gratitude to *the Demon-god* (Shang-te)."[7] But, Mind or Shang-te, as we have seen, is merely the Demiurgic Ruler or second God, who owes his existence and all his powers to the First God, viz, Fate or Reason.

It is obvious then that the reason why the Mind of Man is called God, (神), or the Divinity within us, in the Chinese Classics, is, because it is a portion of the Divine Ether or Light, which is the Rational soul of the Kosmos. Hence the exact parallel between 神, Θεος, and Deus, is unquestionable. "Every ether (soul) in existence, is it not from Heaven? Every body in existence, is it not from Earth?"[8] And when death takes place, "The body and *anima* descend (to Earth), and the Intellect and ether (Rational soul) ascend (to Heaven)."[9] So also in the West: "The mighty Earth and the Ether of Jove, the father of gods and men, generate the human race. What is produced from Earth, goes back again to Earth, and that which springs from ethereal seed, returns to the celestial pole."[10] "Earth is the Mother, she produces the body, Ether adds the soul."[11] "God (the ethereal fire, Jupiter) is the soul of the world."[12] According to Zeno's doctrine, the Minds of Men are parts of God."[13] Cicero calls the Rational soul "God" in the following passage, "Vetet enim

---

1. Enf. i, 64.   2. Cud. i, 371 note.   3. Ibid. p. 475 note.   4. Ibid. p. 354. note.
5. Cud. i, 335, note.   6. Chung Yung, sec. xix.   7. Le Ke, sec. ix.
8. 性理 &c Sec. xxvi, p. 6.   9. Le Yun, i. 20   10. Cud. iii, 279 note.
11. Ibid, p. 280 note.   12. Ibid, i, 211 note.   13. Ibid, ii, p. 107 note.

dominans ille in nobis Deus, injussu hinc nos suo demigrare."¹ "......it is *a common practice* with the Stoics and Platonists to call men gods, as supposing that the sovereign portion of man, namely, the mind and rational soul, emanated from God himself, and is a part of God, and that if man bestows due care on this part, and abstracts it from body, he then becomes wholly like unto God, nay altogether a god."² "Wherefore in order to be consistent, they ought also to have placed all souls among the gods, and to have mutually paid divine honours to each another."³

As the Light or Mind or *Shang-te* is the firstborn God from Chaos;⁴ so also is the Light or Mind or Jupiter of the west, according to Orpheus; "But the Earth being then invisible by reason of the darkness, a light breaking out through the Ether illumined the whole creation ; this light being said by him to be that highest of all beings (before mentioned) which is called also counsel and life."⁵ Hence also *Shang-te* is the same as the Chaldæan Bel or Baal, the Mind of the Kosmos, from whom all other Minds are derived, and who is also said to have formed Light and Darkness or Heaven and Earth, by dividing himself in two.⁶ Confucius says of 太 一 or *Shang-te*, that "he *dividing*, became Heaven and Earth, and gyrating produced Light and Darkness,"⁷ &c.

Lastly, these two Principles are the Sun and Moon. Choo-tsze says, "The Sun and Moon placed in opposition are God and Demon."⁸ "The Light and Darkness placed in opposition are Heaven and Earth, Sun and Moon." "The Light and Darkness are synonymous with the Sun and Moon."⁸ Ching-tsze says, "The Light-Dark Air is Eternal and disperses not, it is the Sun and Moon." He also says "Heaven and Earth, Sun and Moon are the same."¹⁰ &c. "In offering the chief sacrifice, the Great Recompense is made to Heaven (*Shang-te*), and the Sun rules as Lord. He mates with the Moon." "O Sun, O Moon, coming forth from the East, my Father and Mother, who unceasingly nourish me!"¹¹ The Sun and Moon therefore are the Great Father and Mother, or Heaven and his wife Earth, regarded astronmically ; "By the seminal influence of the Sun and Moon the Stars were produced."¹²

So also, "The Persians added the worship of the Moon to that of the Sun, and regarded the Moon as the Sun's wife." "As therefore the Sun was called the god Mithras, so his inseparable companion the Moon, seems to have been called by them the goddess Mithra."¹³ "The prostrations and adorations that are used both by the Greeks and all Barbarians towards the rising and setting Sun and Moon (as well in their prosperities as adversities) declare them to be unquestionably esteemed gods."¹⁴ Philo says, "Wherefore some admiring with a kind of astonishment the nature of both these worlds (*i. e.* invisible ideas and visible bodies) have not only deified the whole of them, but also the most excellent parts in them, as the Sun, and the Moon, and the whole Heaven, which they scruple not at all to call gods."¹⁵ Hammon the chief god of the Egyptians, like *Shang-te*, was also the Sun,¹⁶ as, in fact, was also the chief god of every Pagan system throughout the world. Jupiter, like *Shang-te*, was the great Nous or Mens of Heaven or the Kosmos, and resided in the Sun ; and hence he was thus

---

1. Tusc. Disp. lib. i, cap. xxx ; lxxiv. 2. Cud. i, 373 note. 3. Ibid, ii, 106 note.
4. "Heaven and Earth," par. 6. 5. Cud, i, 503. 6. Ibid, p. 526, Enf. i, 54.
7. Le the. Sec. iv, p. 60. 8. Chung yung sec. xv.
9. Yih King ii, ch. v. Imp. Ed. Com. vi. 上. 10. 性理 &c. xxvii, 1.
11. Odes of I^sel, Sec. iii, Ode. iv. 12. Chin. Rep. iii, 55. 13. Cud, i, 473 note.
14. Ibid, ii, 67. 15. Ibid, pp. 235—6. 16. Ibid, i, 572.

addressed in prayer, "O Omnipotent Sun, the mind and spirit of the whole world."[1] "The 神 of Heaven (soul of *Shang-te*) resides in the Sun, as the 神 of a man resides in his eye." *Kang-he.*

(27.) The Light and Darkness, that is to say the Demon-god *Shang-te* pervades everything in the whole universe, being the principle of life in each. As the twofold soul of each portion of the Kosmos he is invisible, and must not be confounded with grosser matter, in which he is nevertheless inherent and cannot be separated from it.

(28.) The Divine Reason, or Fate, or First God, must not be confounded with *Shang-te* or the Demon-god, that is to say the Light and Darkness, in which, however, He is inherent, and which therefore must not be considered to exist separately from Him.

The latter sentences of this paragraph refer to the opinions of the Taouists, who hold, like the Platonists, that although God and Matter are eternally united together, yet, this union is not absolutely necessary to the existence of the former. This the Confucianists deny, and hold, in common with the Stoics, that this connection is as necessary to the existence of God, as the connection between body and soul is necessary to the existence of Man.

(29, 30, 31.) A reference to part, III. par. 5, 6. will make these paragraphs clear.

(33.) The Light or *Shang-te* is God (神) in virtue of the inherent Fate or Reason, who is the First God. This Light or *Shang-te* is also the Virtuous Nature which Man receives at birth; made to be so, by the inherent Fate; and he is the Great Νοῦς or *Mens* who pervades every portion of his body the world.[2]

---

1. Ibid, ii, p. 162.
2. Compare "Heaven and Earth" par. 20.

SUMMARY.

To sum up: Choo-tsze and the Confucianists in common with the philosophers of Greece and Rome, &c., hold the following tenets: 1.° That the Kosmos or Universe is animated, and they designate it "Heaven." 2.° This Heaven is a Great Man, while Man is a Microcosm, both being made from precisely the same materials, viz., God inherent in Matter. 3.° The Kosmos is compounded of Body and Soul (or Mind), the visible world being the body, of which Heaven is the head and Earth the feet; and the Soul or Mind being also twofold, partly Rational and partly Sentient. 4.° The Mind in Man is the Mind of the Kosmos, being the subtile, Intellectual ether, and being partly Rational and partly Sentient. Man's head also corresponds to Heaven and his feet to Earth, &c. 5.° Heaven is the First Man, and Man is Heaven; or in other words, the First Man or Great Ancestor, Sage, and Sovereign of the whole human race, has *a double character*, viz., Mundane or Divine, and Human. 6.° All Gods are *souls*, and hence images are denounced; while no *personal* God separate from Matter can be found in these systems. 7.° They are Monotheists yet Pantheists, the Divine Reason or First God being a perfect Unity and pervading all things. 8.° The Demiurgic Mind is the *second* God, and is to be carefully distinguished from the First God. 9.° They hold the doctrine "*ex nihilo nihil fit*," and consequently that Matter is eternal. 10.° All give precisely the same titles, and ascribe the same attributes to the First God, who is inherent in the eternal Matter; and lastly, Choo-tsze derives his system from the Yih King, the oldest Chinese Classic in existence.

FINIS.

ERRATA.

Page 18, seventh column, for 成 read 哉
" 32, fourth " omit 奧.
" 84, sixth " for 法 " 去.
" 87, note, " ἀπείϛον " ἀπειρον.
" 102, last " " 恆 " 但.

www.ingramcontent.com/pod-product-compliance
Lightning Source LLC
Chambersburg PA
CBHW020829190426
43197CB00037B/889